Mr. Speaker
James Jerome

Mr. Speaker
James Jerome

McClelland and Stewart

McClelland and Stewart Limited
The Canadian Publishers
25 Hollinger Road
Toronto, Ontario
M4B 3G2

Canadian Cataloguing in Publication Data

Jerome, James.
    Mr. Speaker

Includes index.
ISBN 0-7710-4403-8

1. Jerome, James.   2. Canada–Politics and government–1963-
*3. Canada. Parliament. House of Commons–Biography.
4. Legislators–Canada–Biography.   I. Title.

FC626.J47A3 1985   328.71'092'4   C85-099133-1
F1034.3.J47A3 1985

Printed and bound in Canada

The author would like to acknowledge *The Globe and Mail* for permission to reprint an editorial, which appears in this book in chapter 4.

48,696

Table of Contents

A Canadian historical first: Speaker James Jerome is "dragged" to the Chair by the Leader of the Opposition, Pierre Trudeau (left), and the Prime Minister, Joe Clark (right)—the first time a Canadian Speaker has ever been nominated by two successive prime ministers from opposing political parties.

Introduction

Sometimes, a single event—especially one that we adorn with ceremony—can have personal meaning far beyond the moment and can crystallize so much of what has gone before. In terms of my life, especially the nearly 13 years of it in the House of Commons, six as Speaker, there could be no more appropriate caption for the photograph opposite this page. In fact, the event taking place in the picture does more than bring together some of the past. It represents much of the explanation for having the nerve to begin this book in the first place which, after all, rests on the presumption that what follows is more than just interesting personal experience—that it is actually a bit of history. Even with generous allowances for the usual ego, politicians—at least during their active years—are usually too preoccupied with survival to perceive themselves in this light.

Yet here is this photograph, carried in just about every major newspaper in the country in October, 1979. Thanks to television coverage, introduced during the preceding couple of years, most readers could easily set the scene. The photograph was taken during the opening of Parliament and the election of the Speaker who, as part of some obscure tradition, gives the appearance of being "dragged" to the Chair. The other two men, The Right Honourable Joe Clark and The Right Honourable Pierre Elliott Trudeau, have just changed positions as Prime Minister and Leader of the Opposition following the 1979 general election. With the usual life expectancy of people in these high offices, the chances of them re-appearing in these identical roles after another election are virtually non-existent. But there is more to this photograph. The man in the middle is actually doing this for the *second* time. When we couple that with the change of roles for the other two, then we do have a note of history. In the event, this was indeed the first time a Speaker of the House of Commons had been re-elected after a change of government.

There is one final aspect to the picture that might very well pass unnoticed even among avid Parliament-watchers. Even before the commencement of television coverage of the daily proceedings in the House of Commons, special events, in particular the opening of Parliament, were always covered by the television networks. "Still" cameras, both for tourists and members of the Parliamentary Press Gallery, were always prohibited (and curiously enough were only released from that long-standing prohibition as an indirect consequence of permanent television coverage). As a result, this was the first opening of Parliament to be covered on an official basis by a team of still photographers representing the Press Gallery; so the photograph itself may be something of a collector's item.

But the final give-away is the smile. The man in the middle, the man being "dragged" by the Prime Minister, "kicked" by the Leader of the Opposition, and "digging" in his heels to resist, is nevertheless smiling and there is a very good reason: it has been a fascinating journey—a journey that has taken this man in the middle through all the ups and downs of partisan in-fighting, cliffhanger nominations, election battles lost and won, all leading to the Chair of the House of Commons, an absolutely awesome responsibility, an office and an honour considered to be "in the highest gift of the House of Commons." But in spite of the obvious pressures and frustrations associated with being Mr. Speaker, "the first Commoner," I can honestly say I enjoyed every minute. Perhaps sharing these experiences will provide a similar kind of enjoyment for you.

As I go on to tell you about them, some events will be in chronological sequence but others will not. The emphasis is on those events that memory highlights as being worthy of the telling. This is not a diary, although I must say that in 1974, more than one person suggested that I keep one. I didn't for three reasons: first, I didn't think there was much likelihood that I would do it faithfully and regularly; second, I was very much afraid that I might begin to perform for the diary instead of the other way around; and, finally, the only reason for a diary would be as source material for a book. In 1974, and during all of my years as Speaker, writing a book was something I was absolutely certain I would never do!

There is another reason for this book. The mystique which surrounds our Parliamentary institutions is enormous, and probably the least understood is the Speakership. Members of the House of Commons, especially Cabinet Ministers, operate under relentless time pressure. Many spend years in very effective service, but simply never find the time to develop more than a basic grasp of the concept of the Speakership or the rules of the House. How much less, then, should the average voter understand. And yet there is every reason to believe that television has brought about an impressive increase in the awareness of all Canadians of the process by which we are governed. If so, and if this narrative makes a serious contribution to your understanding of Parliament and the Speakership, I will be rewarded more generously than I deserve.

Acknowledgments

Before getting into my own story, I must tell you about a few other people who played an extremely important part in whatever success I enjoyed as Speaker.

The Clerk of the House of Commons is the resident official with administrative responsibility for virtually everything the Speaker presides over. (Today, the Clerk shares that responsibility with other senior staff members in an administrative committee.) If you look in on the proceedings of the House of Commons, you will see the Clerk seated at the head of the table known as the "Table of the House" immediately in front of the Speaker's Chair. Had you looked in during my first couple of years, there would hardly have been a day that you would not have seen me call the Clerk to my side several times for advice on the dozens of different problems that pop up in the House without warning. Equally, on the more comprehensive procedural debates, where reserved decisions were necessary, he would direct the research and advise on the final ruling. But the Clerk's responsibility at that time went much further. It included final administrative authority for the 3,000 employees and the operational budget which, when I was there, was in the range of one hundred million dollars annually.

In my own case, I was blessed with the presence of Alistair Fraser as Clerk from the time I was first elected in 1974. A lawyer by profession, Alistair served as a special or executive assistant with a number of Cabinet Ministers over a 14-year span from 1951 to 1966 — a period which included both the "Pipeline Debate" and the "Flag Debate" — so he was certainly no stranger to the relationships between Cabinet and Parliament. He was appointed

Clerk Assistant on January 7, 1966, and Clerk of the House of Commons a year and a half later so he had the benefit of over eight years as a master of House procedures before my arrival in 1974. Above all, in all of those responsibilities, he retained a flexibility that very much matched my own approach, and every decision during the 30th Parliament from 1974 to 1979 was prepared with his close cooperation and constant advice. To the extent that my performance during that Parliament merited my re-nomination in 1979, I am forever in his debt because none of it would have gone as well without him.

Upon his retirement in 1979, the office was assumed by the present incumbent, Dr. Beverley Koester. As events transpired, we worked together for only the short life span of the 31st Parliament, and I will have more to say later in the book regarding some changes that we brought about. I also had the benefit of his contributions during the previous two years when he served as Clerk Assistant. From his academic background, he brought an outstanding command of the rationale behind present-day Parliamentary practice, which helped me through some of the very tricky situations in the minority Parliament of 1979.

Most people think the Speaker stays in the Chair for every minute of the proceedings every day. When people praised me for that kind of devotion to duty, I naturally did nothing to discourage them, but the truth is that a Deputy Speaker is elected by the House and he is aided by two assistants. The Deputy Speaker is also designated as Chairman of the Committee of the Whole House. The formal titles of his two assistants are Deputy Chairman and Assistant Deputy Chairman. It is the responsibility of the Deputy Speaker to chair any meetings of the Committee of the Whole House (which sits, for example, to consider clause by clause analysis of any money bills), and also to take responsibility personally, together with his two assistants, for presiding over most of the daily sessions, once the Speaker leaves the Chair following the usual procedural arguments after the daily Question Period. Ordinarily, the Deputy Speaker and his assistants are changed every couple of years, but in my case I had the good fortune during all six years to have the continuous support of Mr. Gerald Laniel (Beauharnois-Salaberry). Many of the procedural problems during my six years originated when he or his assistants were in the Chair. They had the delicate task of dealing with them spontaneously and, in the more serious situations, setting them aside for the following day when I was in the Chair and so that they could be argued after the Members had had a chance to prepare. To Gerald Laniel personally, and to each of the very dedicated Assistant Deputy Speakers who served with him during those six years goes a very special vote of thanks.

On the personal and political side, bear in mind that the Speaker, for all his high profile in Ottawa, must get re-elected back home. When I ran in Sudbury in the general election of 1968, I was carrying on a solo law practice. Long before constituency offices became a part of the support services available to Members, my legal secretary, Karen Christie, was doing that job while she kept the law practice on an even keel. When I stepped down as Speaker and as a Member of Parliament in 1980, she continued on as the constituency office secretary and, as this book goes to press, continues to do so for my successor. I don't think there could be anyone better at the job!

When I began to express interest in moving to Northern Ontario, an Osgoode Hall classmate from Sudbury, Jim Hinds, began to talk about my going there. In the early spring of 1958, he arranged an interview which led to my first position in law practice. From the start he encouraged me to think of politics, but then he did much more. In every campaign he was the first and strongest supporter, doing everything from fund-raising to looking after his own poll. Fittingly, he was the primary organizer of the testimonial dinner which brings this story to a close. Beyond question, without all he did none of the things in this book would have happened.

In 1968, one of the first calls after the election was from a life-long friend and former Conservative Member of Parliament from Toronto, Mr. Arthur Maloney, Q.C. After the usual congratulations, he then recommended his former secretary, Marie Venne. I called her at her home and told her she was hired. She was a bit startled that I didn't want a personal interview, but I told her that if she was good enough for Arthur, she was good enough for me. It turned out that she was a veteran who knew everybody on Parliament Hill on a first-name basis. Many of the thorny constituency problems that I appeared to unravel were really done by her. When Mrs. Venne retired a couple of years later, she brought her niece, Georgie Bracken, into the office. Mrs. Bracken was on maternity leave at the time, and was undecided about the timing of her return to work. Happily, she decided to come back. A successful Member counts more than anything else on people who have a feel for helping others and, whether in respect to the Speaker's responsibilities or to constituency problems, Georgie Bracken's generous attitude in that regard permeated everything I did.

There have been several others who have lent their direct assistance in the preparation of this book. Mr. Philip Laundy was the Director of Research in the Parliamentary Library during all of my years there. He is the author of a very comprehensive book on the Speakers of the Commonwealth, has served, unofficially, as Executive Secretary to the Commonwealth Speakers Conference almost from its inception, and probably knows more about the Speakership than anyone else in the world. I drew great assistance from his texts and also from his scrutiny of the final manuscript before publication.

Mrs. Mary Anne Griffiths has recently been elevated to the position of Clerk Assistant (Research). Almost every scrap of the research material for this book was provided by her or her associates, and without it the book simply could not have been written.

Most of the photographs herein were taken for a book called *Canada's Parliament* which is published under the authority of the Speaker of the House of Commons. It is an excellent volume designed to provide visitors to the Parliament buildings with a high quality souvenir. The project was originally coordinated by Colonel David Currie, V.C., the former Sergeant-at-Arms, and has now been carried forward by the present Sergeant-at-Arms, Major General M.G. Cloutier. The explanatory text in that book was written by Mr. Laundy. The photographs were taken especially for the book by W.G.L. Gibbons in association with Lawson Graphics of Vancouver, and reappear here through their courtesy and cooperation.

The Speaker's staff includes an executive assistant whose primary responsibility is to respond to the needs of individual constituents and, of course, to the constituency as a community. During my six years, that role was filled by three people, Mr. Jim Ovens of Sudbury for one year, Mr. Pierre Guimond for almost two years, and, finally, Mr. David Laballister for the remaining time. David Laballister's background as a radio and television journalist suited him perfectly for the task of maintaining constant communication with everyone in Sudbury, and helping me to do the same. He is presently executive assistant to Mr. Erik Spicer, the Parliamentary Librarian. When I began to run a little flat on this project, he was good enough to return to his former skills and "pump" me for a good deal of the personal material that follows.

Finally, my family—but let me hasten to assure you that this is not the usual perfunctory compliment. Barry (which she steadfastly maintains has always been a great Irish *girl's* name) and I were married on June 25, 1958, and we had four children right away, Mary Lou, Paul, Jim Jr. and Joey. Then, when Joey was ten years old, our fifth and last, Megan, was born on November 26, 1974. Among other things all of this brought quite a number of fresh elements to the Canadian Speakership.

After the opening session of a new Parliament, the Speaker holds a reception for Members, their guests, and a number of officials and dignitaries, including the entire Diplomatic Corps. I rather suspect September 30, 1974 was the first time the Speaker's wife shook hands with them wearing a maternity gown especially designed for the occasion. Two months later when our obstetrician, Dr. Pat Farrell of Sudbury, told me that he was sure about the delivery time, I left Ottawa on the Thursday afternoon after Question Period (the next day was the only sitting day I missed in six years) and arrived at the Sudbury General Hospital just in time to see our new baby arrive. The Speaker's corridor runs along the north end of the Chamber with the portraits of Canadian Speakers since pre-Confederation lining the walls. My best memories of it are of Megan running along it as a three- or four-year-old and giggling when I caught her in my arms. All our children were regulars around those corridors, and most of the staff took a personal interest in their upbringing. I am glad it happened that way because they became the beneficiaries of an education in political science they could never buy at any university.

But above all, my wife's role was enormously important. Barry has a warmth and compassion for people that far exceeds my own, and while it had been amply demonstrated in election campaigns, it really shone through during those six years. The entertainment facilities at the disposal of the Speaker are there in part to receive incoming delegations. But their primary purpose is to bring the Members of the House of Commons together for social occasions, when they can set aside the partisan rivalries and get to know each other a little better. Whether we were doing the annual childrens' Christmas party, a garden party at Kingsmere for a thousand guests, or small dinner parties for new Members and their families on Monday evenings, Barry's personal touch on the hospitality was unmistakable. She made every one of our guests feel at home in a way that I could never have done alone. I am very proud of the role that she, and all my family, played in the events that follow.

1. A Very Unexpected Journey

It would be nice to claim that many of the events in my life came about unexpectedly, but the truth is that until I got into politics, it was exactly the opposite.

When I was in Grade 7 at Our Lady of Perpetual Help School in Moore Park, Toronto, I won a province-wide separate school oratorial contest. From that moment on, I knew how many years I had to go to high school, university, and Osgoode Hall before becoming a lawyer. Along the way, I pursued public speaking at high school and at the University of Toronto, although, typically, I spent more time trying to play hockey–at which I was not nearly as gifted. In first year at Osgoode Hall, I was successful in the Moot Court Competition. It seemed that courtroom practice was in the cards for me from the very beginning, and that is exactly how I spent my first 15 years in practice after graduation in 1958.

It was the same with our marriage. I first met Barry when we were in Grade 12, and we went together for ten years before we were married. In my final year, when I was president of the St. Michael Student Council, she was head girl at St. Joseph's Convent School. Where I was active in debating, she was involved in public relations work, first as a member of Eaton's Junior Council and later in a full-time public relations career with Eaton's– working as a senior coordinator with the same council and as a fashion consultant. Barry has always had the kind of personal warmth to suit her perfectly for that kind of career. She also has the kind of dedication that makes it natural for her to stay with the task at hand until it is finished. It is a perfect script for a future politician, but during all of those years, neither of us had any contact with politics at any level.

The only unpredictable part was moving to Sudbury. It came about when I began to get this notion in 1956 to get away from the huge Metropolitan Toronto area and go some place where we could have a greater sense of personal involvement in the community. Until the summer of 1957, however, I was still quite sure that our future would be in Toronto. But during that summer, I spent ten weeks as an articling student with a law firm in Sault Ste. Marie. The first morning, I found myself walking to work through a quiet residential neighbourhood and getting there in less than ten minutes. I simply couldn't believe it. Then, when a friend invited me out to his cottage for a swim at lunch and we were back before 2 o'clock, it really turned my head. A couple of days later, when I left the office at 5 o'clock and was on the first tee at 5:15, I was sold! I knew I was headed for Northern Ontario. The only question was where. Then, six months later, I was on my way to Sudbury for an interview with a couple of good friends from our graduating year. Barry and I were married on June 7, and I began practising with Miller, Maki and Inch in Sudbury on June 16, 1958.

It was still almost five years later before I took my first active role in politics when I became president of the Sudbury Young Liberal Association. I knew that I probably wouldn't be content going through life without having at least one good try at the political life, but I had no plan in mind and certainly no definite target. In September 1965, in a coffee shop across from the courthouse where a good many of the lawyers used to gather, I was astounded to hear that there would be an acclamation for a couple of City Council seats, and that in my own ward there were only the two incumbents running for the two seats. I thought about it all day long. With nominations set to close in only 48 hours, I made a quick decision. We gathered a few friends, filed the papers, and threw together a campaign team. The strategy had to be simple. There was no money for radio or television advertising. Even if there had been, it is not practical when you are only running in one-sixth of the city. But as simple as it was, it remains effective to this day. We developed one theme. I wanted to instill some optimistic or positive thinking on Sudbury City Council. We printed my name and that simple message, so we could leave it with every voter. Then we set out to take it personally to every door in the ward. We headed the poll and, less than two weeks after that conversation in the coffee shop, I was a member of the 1966-67 Sudbury City Council.

Even with that, my entry into federal politics came about as a surprise. During those years, Sudbury was represented in Ottawa by Roger Mitchell, a pharmacist and long-time Liberal Member, and at Queen's Park by the outspoken and brilliant orator and lawyer, Elmer Sopha, also a Liberal. As in most communities, lawyers were active in politics. Several of them were considered to be the rightful successor to Mr. Mitchell, who was getting up in years and was in failing health. At the same time, redistribution created a new provincial riding of Sudbury-East, and Mr. Sopha took on the responsibility of bringing about the first riding association. He called several meetings to which I was invited. Over the course of the next few weeks, everyone was given a specific responsibility, except me. When I asked him about it, he said that he was hoping I would seek the nomination! It was the first time that a career other than in municipal politics had ever entered my head. I asked him about his own plans. He said he thought that if Roger Mitchell were to step down, he would seek the federal nomination. That seemed natural enough to me, but before I had too much time to think about it, a number of other things happened rather quickly.

An Ontario Liberal convention was scheduled in January of 1967, at the Royal York Hotel in Toronto. I was a delegate. While a number of us were on our way to Toronto for the meeting, we learned that Roger Mitchell had passed away. Most of us quickly made plans to come back early from the convention to attend the funeral. More news awaited us when we arrived at the Royal York. A radio news team covering the convention saw our Sudbury identification badges and asked me what I thought about Mr. Sopha's announcement. I asked the reporter to turn off the microphone for a minute so that he could tell me what it was that Mr. Sopha had said. Naturally, I was surprised to hear that after a discussion with his Party Leader at Queen's Park, Mr. Robert Nixon, Mr. Sopha had committed himself to staying on as part of the provincial team. As a result, the nomination for the by-election created by Mr. Mitchell's death was wide open.

At that time, the constitution for the Sudbury Federal Liberal Association called for a closed nominating convention, consisting of approximately one delegate for each polling subdivision in the previous election and a few others. As I recall, the number came to 212. The by-election was actually held in May of 1967, the nomination about two months earlier, in March. Here again, the simplest but most direct campaign strategy was the one that worked. There were four candidates for the nomination, but I knew I was the only one who paid a personal visit to each delegate, and in each case I took with me someone who knew the delegate personally. I also worked very hard to include some French remarks in my nominating speech because Sudbury is over 30 per cent French-speaking. I was pleased with the way it went at the convention, but no one will ever convince me that it was as important as that preliminary personal contact.

The by-election campaign was tough. The Sudbury seat had been held by a Liberal member from the beginning, but there was at this time a great deal of disenchantment with the Pearson-Diefenbaker squabble in Parliament. There was also a very optimistic mood among the highly organized New Democrats, who were enjoying increasing support from the Sudbury local of the steelworkers' union – at that time the biggest in Canada. The prediction was that we would lose by a few thousand votes, but we ran a very energetic campaign nevertheless. It was not uncommon for us to start at 6 a.m., at the gates of one of the mines, and still be out knocking on doors at 9 o'clock at night. One night I knocked on a man's door just at 9 o'clock, and it made my day to hear that miner say: "You must be really trying, I saw you at 6 o'clock this morning." During the campaign, the Hon. Paul Martin, who was then Secretary of State for External Affairs, telephoned the house twice to wish me well. Both calls were before 7 a.m., and Barry took the greatest of pleasure in being able to tell him that I was already out campaigning. We made some mistakes in that campaign and alienated some of the old guard, something that I could only learn by experience. In the end, we lost by 156 votes, less than one vote per poll, but I used that experience in every campaign after that. Whenever we thought it wasn't worth knocking on one more door, it always gave us something to think about.

A year later when Trudeaumania was sweeping the country, everybody was after a Liberal nomination. Naturally, I thought I had earned the right to one in Sudbury without contest. What a pipe dream! The first thing that happened was that the Mayor, a long-time Conservative, indicated his intention to seek the Liberal nomination. He had a number of supporters within the Liberal Association, but a great many were incensed at an outsider suddenly coming in. The executive proposed to amend the constitution by requiring any candidate for the nomination to prove membership in the Liberal Association for 90 days. Obviously, acceptance of such a proposal by the Association as a whole would end the Mayor's chances. To give you some idea of the intensity of the ensuing battle, the meeting to resolve the constitutional question was attended by over 1,000 people. The executive proposal was adopted by a majority of about two to one, and so ended that challenge. The nominating meeting was announced for the following week and, lo and behold, one of those senior lawyers who had always been considered the natural successor to Mr. Mitchell in the first place, but who had not entered the nomination race for the by-election a year earlier, then announced his intention to contest the nomination. We were back a week later with another 1,500 people present, and I was able to carry the nomination by about the same margin of two to one. I was beginning to learn that in politics your enemies can't harm you nearly as much as your friends! Happily, the 1968 election was a breeze, and I enjoyed a 10,000 vote majority—which stayed pretty well constant during the entire time I was a Member in Ottawa.

As I mentioned in the acknowledgments, one of the first things I did after the election was to hire Marie Venne as my secretary, and the first thing I asked her to do was to try to find a place for me to live. A couple of weeks later, when she said that she had found two or three interesting-looking spots, I headed for Ottawa to be sworn in. Marie and her son Edgar met me at the airport, and we headed for one of the apartments she had picked out. It was only when we got out of the car to walk into the apartment building that we all realized I had left the airport without thinking about my suitcase. You don't suppose I was excited?

Actually the excitement never totally subsided for me. The first two-day post-election caucus was a great thrill—getting the chance to spend so much time with prominent Members of Cabinet, who, up until then, I had only known from a distance. There was also, of course, a chat with the Prime Minister. It was very heady stuff. I can remember one of the instructional sessions arranged for new Members, which were then conducted by the political parties (they are now done by the House administration). It was about how to prepare and file private Member's legislation. At that point, I was still trying to figure out some of the basics of being on the Hill, and I was still excited about long-distance privileges, free postage for constituents to write, things like that.

The next thing I recall is being told about the option for Members to serve on various committees. One of my preferences, of course, was Justice and Legal Affairs, but I knew that seniority would rule that out. There was one assignment that I thought wouldn't be the subject of a lot of competition. The Standing Committee on Procedure and Organization was about to embark on a complete revision of the Standing Orders of the House. In all of my years of law practice, I could hold my own before any judge or jury, but detailed preparation, and especially rules and regulations, had never been my great strength. So in a sense, I expressed interest in the assignment in spite of myself, really because I knew that I would never take the trouble to develop a solid understanding of the rules unless I got myself involved in a project of this sort. I also had an ulterior motive. The spearhead of the Trudeau leadership campaign in Ontario had been The Hon. Donald S. Macdonald. It was quite clear, even at that early stage, that he would be the number one English-speaking Cabinet Minister, certainly in Ontario, and perhaps in Cabinet. He had agreed to serve in his first two years as Government House Leader and therefore, as is customary, was given the position of President of the Privy Council. Revision of the Standing Orders would therefore be his project, and if I was going to work together closely with anyone in the Cabinet, I couldn't think of a better choice.

One of the unexpected benefits on that committee was that the membership from the other parties was at the highest level, consisting of their most distinguished veteran Members. It also immediately opened my eyes to Parliament at its best and at its worst. I don't intend to go through all of the Standing Orders in detail, of course, but the essential proposal of the committee was to make two extremely significant changes in House procedure. The groundwork for these changes, which were adopted on a permanent basis at the end of 1968, had been laid by a Special Committee on Procedure and Organization appointed in 1964 under the chairmanship of Speaker MacNaughton. This committee included a former Speaker, Marcel Lambert, and the Deputy Speaker, Lucien Lamoureux, who later became Speaker.

The first change had to do with supply. During the first couple of meetings, it was the constant source of discussion, so much so that I was embarrassed to ask anyone to explain it to me. It gets its name from the process by which Parliament supplies money to Her Majesty for the running of the country. Whereas the budget and the budget bills are about raising money, the supply process concerns spending. It begins with a tabling of Government spending estimates in Parliament, which are contained in what is known as the "Blue Book." Scrutiny is Parliament's most fundamental responsibility. It is equally the most basic right of the individual Member to withhold approval of the ultimate supply bill until such time as the Government has brought forth satisfactory responses to any grievances. That was the principle upon which the first Parliament was formed, and it is as important today as it was then. At that time, Ministers were questioned about their spending estimates in the Committee of Supply—a Committee of the Whole House. Essentially control of that process was in the hands of the Opposition.

The proposal before the Procedure Committee in the fall of 1968 was to make two changes: first, to refer all spending estimates (and almost all legislation) for scrutiny to the various standing committees of the House, instead of being restricted to one Committee of the Whole; second, to fix a date for the termination of the process by putting the supply bill through all three readings if necessary. Since the previous supply process had always been looked upon as an opportunity for Opposition Members to air their grievances, it was also proposed to allot up to 25 sitting days, to be known as Opposition days, on which the motion to be debated would be entirely at the discretion of the Opposition—six of them potentially leading to votes of want of confidence in the Government.

I don't want to create the impression that such a massive change was accepted easily or universally—far from it. When I say it was Parliament at its best, it is because of the enlightened discussion in the committee, the formation of consensus about those areas which each caucus would accept, and the agreement that it was necessary for dissenters on all sides to have time to debate it in the House. But after all of that had been arranged, the following summer the House accepted the changes. They are now House of Commons practice.

It was the other major proposal that brought out the worst: CLOSURE—the very word raises the hair on the neck of Parliamentarians all around the world. And yet it is generally conceded that the Standing Order must contain a provision which will permit the Government to close off debate, so long as it is prepared to take the political responsibility for doing so. The old closure rule is one that can be invoked only when the debate is under way (really it is to permit the closing off of a debate that has either gone on too long, or threatens to). Even with that limited application, every time it has been used, certainly in Canada, it has met with outrage as another example of the Government trampling on the rights of the Opposition. In this case, the new proposal on closure was to arm the Government with a much greater power: to allocate specific time for any stage of a bill before debate began.

Plain and simply, the Opposition reaction was wild! There was no consensus in the committee, and after two months of work, the package was debated briefly in the House of Commons before the Christmas recess. The House accepted most of the other changes after some discussion, but violently rejected any suggestion of specific time allocation. When the House rose for Christmas recess, there was no hope of any approval. After the recess, the House turned its attention to other business until summer. Then, just before the House was *hoping* to rise at the end of June for the summer break, another motion for approval of the committee's report was introduced. The idea that progress would be made in two or three days during the remainder of that month was a pious hope indeed. As invariably happened at that time, the House went on well into July—in a bitter, very acrimonious debate. So much so that when I went home, I was sure I would get a lot of complaints about the bickering and the vicious tones of the discussions. It was a great eye opener for me when the first few people I met asked how I was enjoying the summer recess, now that the House was not sitting! Finally, the Government had to invoke the old closure rule to force a vote on the new rule, and the motion was carried by the Government majority. It was a far cry from Parliament at its best, but in the years to follow, the rule (75A, 75B, and 75C) was resorted to quite infrequently, and I think, on balance, it worked rather well.

24

The highlight of my second year as a Member was my first trip outside of Canada. I was elected as a delegate to the Commonwealth Parliamentary Association Conference in Australia. Although we could ill afford the trip at the time, I knew we would never have another chance, so we scraped together the money for the round-trip fare for Barry, and we had an unbelievable three weeks in Australia. Just as the conference was coming to a close, we received a telephone call from the Prime Minister, who told me that for the last two years of that Parliament he was going to designate me as a Parliamentary Secretary. Then he said: "Jim, before you get too excited, you're going to be with the Government House Leader." We both knew that unlike the travel and high profile involved with other Ministries, mine would tie me to the House virtually every sitting day. The Prime Minister also told me that since Donald Macdonald's first two years had included the extra heavy assignment of procedural reform, he was anxious to move to another portfolio. Happily, The Hon. Allan MacEachen had agreed to return once again as Government House Leader.

In the short run, there was a slight disadvantage. Mr. MacEachen was hoping to spend a good deal of that month helping out in a provincial election in Nova Scotia, and they were both anxious that I get home as soon as possible, although they were not insisting. I was on the next plane. In the long run, however, I simply could not have hoped to work with a better House Leader. Allan MacEachen had then served almost 20 years in Parliament, and there were never more than a handful who could match him in his knowledge of rules and procedure. When you added in his skill as a strategist, negotiator, and debater, then you had a Parliamentary Leader in a class by himself. His personal preference, moreover, was to have his Parliamentary Secretaries take on as much responsibility as they felt they could handle.

The routine responsibilities of a Parliamentary Secretary to the Government House Leader have always involved a coordinating role with each Minister and with the Party Whip, to ensure that the right Members are in the House at the right times so that the Government programme runs smoothly through debates and votes. The responsibilities also included coordinating replies to the several hundred written questions and demands for papers filed each session (and as a pre-determined regular agenda item, advising the House whether they should be answered or deferred for debate); overseeing Government participation on the two to three times a week the House considers any private Members' bills or motions; and playing a similar role in what has been dubbed affectionately "The Late Show," which is, incidentally, one of Parliament's most meaningful practices—especially for the backbench Member. Any Member of Parliament dissatisfied with answers received during Question Period may request that the matter be raised again in the daily adjournment debate. The fact is that the House rules provide for automatic adjournment without debate at a certain time each day. Instead, the Speaker advises the House that it will consider up to three such questions on a precise allocation of three minutes per question and seven minutes for the reply, generally delivered by the Parliamentary Secretary to the appropriate Minister, or by me since I had to be there anyway.

All of this constituted a pretty full plate, but as soon as I seemed able to keep it on an even keel, I was immediately encouraged to do more. Virtually every day, Question Period was followed by a barrage of procedural dog fights. Mr. MacEachen's preference was to leave for his office. I would have to deflect, defuse, or defend as the case might be. I was to re-call him only if something seemed critical. He took me with him as an observer to meetings of the Cabinet Committee on Planning and Priority, so I would be aware of the longer range legislative agenda. He also had me attend every meeting of the House Leaders. These were held as needed, which is to say at least every week, and sometimes daily in times of crisis. They are informal meetings, with no fixed agenda, and are only referred to by inference in one or two of the house rules. But the fact is that virtually nothing of importance occurs in Parliament without their prior approval.

Finally, and somewhat prophetically, Mr. MacEachen often sent me to represent him when the Speaker invited the House Leaders to lunch or dinner, which took place three or four times in each session. These meetings generally helped all concerned in reaching consensus to deal with any number of the Speaker's many problems—from procedural storm-clouds to M.P.s' support services, and on through the enormous and almost entirely unknown administrative responsibilities of running the House of Commons as an ongoing operation. At the end of that Parliament

26

(1972), I don't think I had to defer to more than four or five very experienced Members in terms of understanding the House of Commons!

It is very hard to remember how long I had been a Member of Parliament before the idea of being Speaker first entered my head. The 28th Parliament, my first, ran from 1968-72, and it certainly was not during those four years. When new Members first arrive in Ottawa, they are somewhat overwhelmed at having triumphed against impossible odds. In various states of ecstasy and shock at their success and at the fantastic experiences that lie ahead of them, they tend to consider the occupant of the Chair almost as part of the House itself. So much so that the first time newly elected Members actually see the Speaker when he is not dressed in the formal garb of the Chamber, they are often caught a bit by surprise. This aura that surrounds the Speaker is enhanced by his mastery of House rules, which no one else seems to understand, and by the respect which he commands from the more senior Members. Indeed, it is difficult to picture the House without the Speaker being there.

This was very much my view of my predecessor, the Hon. Lucien Lamoureux, who was truly one of Canada's most distinguished Speakers. There simply was never any thought that he might one day move on and be replaced. That I might be the one to replace him was beyond any semblance of reality.

The 1972 campaign was certainly a far different experience for the Liberal Party nationally than it had been in 1968. The result was that The Hon. Robert Stanfield came within one seat of forming the Government. The Trudeau plurality was so slim that there was a serious question as to whether he could begin to govern. When he did, and after he announced his Cabinet, I, along with the 70 other Members overlooked, did what Members of Parliament have been doing since time immemorial. I sought out my senior Minister, Donald Macdonald, to find out how a seemingly intelligent man like our Prime Minister could perpetuate such a grievous oversight! Please understand that every candidate feels that he or she will be elected, and once elected, that their party should govern, that they belong of course in the Cabinet—and that once in the Cabinet, they are a great choice for future Prime Minister. . . . Let me assure you that this phenomenon is as close to universal truth as there is in political life.

27

The chorus of such backbench pleas falls on a leader's ears like an endless litany.

So I put my case. As a region, Northern Ontario consisted of 13 seats and, with only one Cabinet Minister for that vast area, I felt we were underrepresented. While the party had lost seats in the rest of the country, all of us had been returned in Northern Ontario, so it was obvious that the region deserved a second, if not a third Member in Cabinet. This complaint by backbench Members is so routine that I wouldn't bother with it here, except that it had a small part to play in my ultimately becoming Speaker. The Minister, who of course couldn't give me much more than a sympathetic ear, raised the possibility of me serving as Deputy Speaker. It was an idea that had never occurred to me and I was taken completely by surprise. My immediate reaction ranged from cautious to negative, but I asked for a day or two to give it some thought. As it happened, I was sharing a suite of offices with Hugh Faulkner (Peterborough), who had served with great distinction as Deputy Speaker in 1971-72, and he was very helpful. (The position of Deputy Speaker has existed since 1885, and the Standing Orders provide that the Deputy Speaker shall be required to possess the full and practical knowledge of the official language which is not that of Mr. Speaker.)

In the end, I couldn't put aside two concerns: that the appointment might be perceived in Sudbury as having all of the constraints imposed upon the Speaker without the corresponding authority; and that it would be seen as a first step in the direction of the Chair as opposed to Cabinet—a choice that I most emphatically did not want to make! So when Donald Macdonald and I returned to the subject, I declined, but our meetings had planted a seed that made me think about the Chair for the very first time. They also had another important effect. We concluded, at my request, with a discussion of my nomination as a committee chairman. My preference was for Justice. As it turned out, the opportunity to serve in that capacity during the following two years not only provided a special measure of satisfaction, but in its own way drew me one step closer to the Chair.

On the Justice Committee, we were once again favoured with outstanding membership. The Conservative delegation included three former provincial Attorneys-General: Claude Wagner of Quebec, Allan Lawrence of Ontario, and Gordon Fairweather of

New Brunswick, now Canada's first Human Rights Commissioner. The Government team included Mark MacGuigan, later Minister of Justice, and J.J. Blais, later Solicitor-General. The two N.D.P. Members, John Gilbert of Toronto and Stuart Leggatt of Vancouver, were lawyers of independent mind and sound judgment based on many years of experience in active general practice.

We considered two very important bills: the "Wiretap Bill," and a bill to extend the ban on capital punishment. I could likely write a whole book on those two subjects alone, but I want to confine it here to the amendments to the capital punishment bill because they had an effect on my ultimate nomination as Speaker.

The purpose of the bill was not to deal in any substantive way with capital punishment, but merely to extend the expiry date of the first five-year ban from that year, 1973, to 1978. During our deliberations, the then Solicitor-General, The Hon. Warren Allmand, produced a series of proposed amendments, with Cabinet approval, which he obviously was only able to obtain after the bill had been introduced: to redefine life imprisonment and eliminate capital punishment entirely. I have always been opposed to capital punishment and so were several of the committee members, so support for the principle was not the problem. In fact, it is now the law as a result of a bill passed in the subsequent Parliament when I was in the Chair. The problem was procedural and it was very serious. A discussion immediately arose as to how such sweeping changes to the substantive law could be made as an incidental amendment to this very limited kind of bill. After extensive argument, I took the question under consideration for decision at the next meeting. I sought out Mr. Speaker Lamoureux, who quite properly told me, as I later did many times, that since he might have to rule on any attempt the Government might make to re-introduce these clauses when the bill ultimately came back on the floor of the House, it would be improper for him to suggest any precise decision on my part. It did not occur to me to discuss it with Warren, whom I knew very well, or with other Ministers, whom I saw every day.

On June 28, 1973, I ruled the proposed amendments out of order. It was not, as you can imagine, an event that escaped attention. It also certainly cleared away any doubts about my impartiality. I must add that neither then nor at any time after did

I have any reason to feel that the ruling created any personal hostility within the Liberal ranks. I also took some comfort from the fact that in due course, when the bill was reported out of our committee back to the House, an attempt was made to present the same amendments there. Speaker Lamoureux, however, ruled that the Minister was unable to do so on procedural grounds.

Not long after, rumours began about my being the next Speaker. They really gathered momentum after the Government was defeated in 1974 and Lucien Lamoureux announced that he would not contest the election in Stormont-Dundas. Election day was July 8, 1974, and Prime Minister Trudeau was returned to a majority position of 141 seats. During the August 1 civic holiday, I came home on Saturday afternoon to learn of an urgent call from The Hon. Mitchell Sharp in Ottawa. When the Secretary of State for External Affairs is contacting Members of Parliament in August, you think in terms of an invitation to dinner in honour of a visiting Head of State. But when I returned the call, his opening words were: "Make sure you're sitting down, because I have to first tell you what the Prime Minister has asked me to take on before you will understand this call." We shared some banter about his choice as Government House Leader, a responsibility for which he felt entirely unprepared, emotionally or technically—but which he discharged with his customary excellence through 1974 and 1975. In that capacity, of course, the purpose of his call was less of a surprise: it was a preliminary exploration of my reaction to a possible nomination as Speaker.

We gathered everyone immediately—family, friends, key members of our election team—and we talked it over well into the night. Finally, Barry, as she had done so many times before, injected some common sense into the frenetic political merry-go-round: "This is not a decision that can be made in comparison with something else. It is an absolutely singular responsibility, not something anyone outside the House of Commons fully understands. Jim, you have to decide in a positive way if it's something you want to do." Indeed, our focus had been completely on the negative side. We were worried that our voters would see it as a muzzle, tying my hands behind my back—and maybe it would be so. Personally, it would mean abandonment forever of ambition for upward mobility in politics, which went directly against every instinct that got me into politics in the first place. At the same time, however, I had been greatly impressed with the way Speaker Lamoureux had discharged his responsibilities, and with the respect all Members had for him and for the Chair. I was always more at ease when partisan hostility gave way to intelligent compromise, and I felt sure I would be comfortable protecting and balancing the rights of all Members in that kind of process. More and more, it seemed that, unplanned, all the events I have just described had a direction: the work on the procedural committee, Parliamentary Secretary to the Government House Leader, and chairmanship of the Justice Committee. More and more, I became fascinated with the idea, excited by the challenge. When the last guest left, I think we knew that if the Prime Minister could ease our concerns, I would do it!

The next day, I called Mitchell, and later the call came through from the Prime Minister. When he made the offer, I had the impression he expected me to accept over the phone. Once assured that I was not asking for a meeting just to say no, he quickly agreed to meet for lunch at 24 Sussex after a Cabinet meeting arranged for Tuesday morning. If you have never been in Ottawa in August, you don't know what heat and humidity really mean. Of course, I was in shirt, tie, and suit and, of course, the Prime Minister emerged from Cabinet in T-shirt and sandals. As he jumped behind the wheel of his treasured convertible Mercedes, my jacket and tie were in the back seat before we were in gear. We stopped at Parliament's Wellington Street exit, and he cursed at not being able to make a left turn! Before I even had time to smile, the two secret service cars had traffic stopped in both directions: couldn't there have been someone on the spot with a camera?

During lunch, the Prime Minister's answers were direct and thorough. In terms of individual constituents, he confirmed that the Speaker has extra staff to ensure the best possible service. In terms of the constituency as a whole, obviously no Member, Minister or otherwise, sees much to be gained by antagonizing the one who presides over every meeting of the House. But more than that, it was his view that no Member should be embarrassed in front of his constituents by virtue of his service as Speaker, so Cabinet should always meet the Speaker's reasonable requests. Obviously, the emphasis had to be on "reasonable," but he backed it with his personal commitment to intervene if I felt that Sudbury's needs were not being fairly met by any of his Ministers. In terms of my own future, he did not disagree that this probably was a step that would lead me out of political life—but neither did he think that any Prime Minister should be expected to write a blank cheque so that even the most disgraceful performance in office might call for some reward negotiated in advance. On the other hand, he had responded fully to the requests of my predecessor who had been appointed to the Diplomatic Corps in Brussels only weeks earlier. Moreover, and perhaps more significantly, he was then in the process of considering a judicial appointment in Nova Scotia for Robert McCleave, a Conservative Member who had served for two years as Deputy Speaker. How much more so then, should he be expected to be forthcoming in respect to an appointment for a retiring Speaker.

Fair enough: my objections were fully answered. I am sure he was surprised when I asked for time to think about it. His reasons were plausible: he was in the process of selecting his Cabinet for the new Parliament and, as a matter of propriety, felt that the selection of his candidate for Speaker should be announced first. Furthermore, by doing it that way, he avoided any impression that his candidate for Speaker had been chosen only from among those he had rejected as Cabinet Ministers. We agreed to meet again at 4 o'clock, at which time I thought I could probably give him a final answer. One more call home and that was it.

At 4 o'clock, when I went back to tell the Prime Minister of my decision, he began to gather the people who would normally be involved in handling the matter from then on. But about half his staff had taken off the only days likely to be available to them for a bit of summer vacation. In particular, Joyce Fairbairn (now Senator), Special Assistant to the Prime Minister in matters relating to Parliament, was away on holiday. The result was that a press officer came in, and we simply ran over whether the announcement could be released right away. Of course, as far as I was concerned it was fine. In fact, I had one eye on the clock because the small airline I had come down on during the holiday weekend had a flight going back in about an hour's time, and I was anxious to be in Sudbury as soon after the announcement as possible. I left almost immediately, ran to my office to tell my staff the news, and then dashed to the airport. On the plane, I was a jumble of emotions. I had a great sense of relief that all of the discussion and handwringing had finally ended, that the decision had been made—but more than that, I had a sense of pure exhilaration that I can only remember two or three times in my entire life. It was the right choice!

We expected a stir, but I don't think anyone was ready for a volcano. Every representative of the news media was at the airport in teams of twos and threes. This time they were not just there for the usual 30-second interview for local consumption; they all had national or international assignments. From that moment on, our lives were catapulted into national prominence that stayed with us until 1980. The next few days were absolute bedlam. Everybody at both my constituency and Ottawa offices, and at our home, hardly did anything else except deal with requests for photo sessions, interviews, background material, and so on.

In politics, the higher you fly, the harder you hit when you come down and, in this case, it didn't take long. Within a couple of days of the announcement from the Prime Minister's office, one came in turn from the office of The Hon. Robert Stanfield, Leader of the Opposition. He deeply regretted the Prime Minister's failure to consult him in the selection of the candidate for Speaker, which he considered to be an impropriety of considerable dimension. Normally, he would have been pleased to have seconded the nomination on the opening day of Parliament and therefore to encourage all Opposition Members to join in making the vote unanimous. Under the circumstances, he would have to discuss the matter with his caucus to find out what course they should follow. His announcement also pointed out that the question of principle had nothing to do with the particular choice in this instance, with which he could find no fault.

In fairness to Mr. Stanfield, there was more than simple courtesy at stake. The Speaker is not appointed, of course, he is elected by all Members of Parliament on opening day. Section 44 of The British North America Act (now the Constitution Act) provides that the House of Commons on first assembling after a general election shall proceed with all practical speed to elect one of its Members to be Speaker. Without that election, it is an unwarranted assumption to consider anyone as Speaker-elect. He was making the point that the Speaker's role, as guardian of the rights of all Members on an equal basis, should be emphasized through the seconding of the nomination by the Leader of the Opposition. As well, he felt that there should have been not only formal advance consultation, but possibly a joint press announcement. Incidentally, the British avoid this problem by having the nominating Member and the seconder from the backbenches on opposite sides of the House.

In fairness to Mr. Trudeau, I don't think these Parliamentary niceties crossed his mind on the day he and I discussed the Speakership. Normally, it would have been something on which he would have taken direction from senior staff who were away on holidays. In addition, there had been considerable talk around Parliament and in the press about my possible appointment, and there was some justification for the Prime Minister in simply considering the announcement as confirmation of something that had been expected for some time.

For my part, it was typical of political life: give you the world in the morning and take it away in the afternoon. The whole thing was now plunged into great uncertainty, which was not resolved until the opening of Parliament almost two months later. Right up until the very last moment, I thought there was every possibility that during the actual election something might be said or done which would lead me to feel that the choice was not unanimous, and that as a matter of honour I might be required to reject the nomination. Thank Heaven it didn't happen!

On September 30, 1974, the Prime Minister moved, seconded by The Hon. President of the Privy Council (Mr. Mitchell Sharp), that "James Jerome, Esquire, member for the electoral district of Sudbury do take the Chair in this House as Speaker." In the process, he made a number of very complimentary remarks, and interestingly enough included these two sentences: "But Mr. Jerome's contribution as Chairman of the Justice Committee was also remarkable. In that capacity, he demonstrated not only his legal expertise and political ability, but also his fair-mindedness in difficult situations, where no partisan pressure could make him alter the decisions he felt were well-founded."

The Hon. Mr. Stanfield, as Leader of the Opposition, was the next to speak, and he dealt with his decision not to formally second the motion in the following words:

> Following the election of July and prior to the calling of this
> session I read in the press that the Prime Minister would

propose Mr. Jerome's name as Speaker, but there was no consultation, no prior knowledge, despite any suggestions in the press to the contrary. There is no need here to go into the details or to take you, Mr. Fraser, or the House through a controversy between the Prime Minister and myself following the announcement of the Prime Minister's intention. There was no consultation. In my judgment, in the absence of such consultation, this was a substantial step backward from the position we had achieved through 1968 and 1972.

Mr. Fraser, I can hardly exaggerate my personal disappointment at this turn of events. In these circumstances, as I told the Prime Minister, I could not second the nomination of Mr. Jerome. Mr Jerome, of course, will receive the full cooperation of myself and members of my party as he discharges his difficult and very important responsibilities of presiding over this House. I hope, as the Prime Minister has indicated here this morning, that we can again take up the question of achieving a permanent Speakership totally removed from partisan politics once a Speaker has been chosen for this high office by this House.

Incidentally, the reference in Mr. Stanfield's speech to Mr. Fraser comes about because the opening of a new Parliament is the only time when there is no Speaker in the Chair to whom remarks can be addressed. It is also the only time that anyone else except an elected Member can address the House directly. When the House assembles, it is the duty of the Clerk (then Alistair Fraser) to inform the House that, there being no one in the Chair, it must immediately proceed to the election of a Speaker. Until the Speaker is actually elected, responses may be addressed to the Clerk.

Some further kind words were contributed by Mr. Ed Broadbent (Oshawa), Leader of the New Democratic Party, and Mr. Réal Caouette (Témiscamingue), Leader of the Social Credit Party. Happily, the vote was unanimous. It was very much as Parliament should be. The disagreement between the Prime Minister and the Leader of the Opposition involved an important matter of principle, and it was raised with the prominence it deserved. But the election of the Speaker, and in particular sending him on his way with the goodwill of all Members, was even more important. As so often happens, the House found the right way to do justice to both positions. For me, it marked an enormous milestone on a very unexpected journey.

2. The Parliamentary Tradition

Finally, the uncertainty was over! With great relief, I was "dragged" to the Chair by The Right Honourable Pierre Elliott Trudeau and The Honourable Mitchell Sharp. Of course, I couldn't have presumed upon the election result, especially before the clarification of the position the Conservative Party had taken. But like the full set of robes and the tricorn hat tailored to my measurements and hanging at that moment in the Speaker's change-room, I had to have an acceptance speech ready. The Hansard for September 30, 1974, records these as my first words to the House from the Chair:

> Hon. members, I beg to return my humble acknowledgements to the House for the great honour you have been pleased to confer on me by choosing me to be your Speaker.
>
> If those words sound familiar, it is because they have been said here by Speakers for the last 100 years or so, and for many hundreds of years in other parliaments. Perhaps it is an appropriate way for every Speaker to begin, because if you start to tinker and tamper with the traditional way of doing things, the lesson you learn is that no matter how you try to modify or improve tradition it has a certain value which perhaps you did not fully appreciate when you first looked at such a simple sentence. When you try to put it in your own words it does not come out as well, no matter how you try to change it; so perhaps there is a lesson that some of the traditions are more than just traditions but have other values attached to them. Perhaps that is a proper subject for a new Speaker to think about as he begins his task.

There is honour, of course, in being a member of the House of Commons. It is an honour that we all share, a very special honour conferred upon us by those who are the final judges in our democratic system. It is a great honour to be a member of the House of Commons, but to receive a favourable judgment from the members themselves is an even greater honour which perhaps only the members of the House of Commons can fully understand. Sometimes the work we do here appears to be a battle for individual advantage or party advantage. But all of us realize that what is done here is extremely important work on behalf of all the people of Canada, not only for their individual rights but, in addition to that, is an example to all the people of Canada that change must be brought about through the process of law and order in a proper, democratic way. So, every meeting we hold here should be an example to our people.

To be given the honour to preside over these important meetings, and obviously the session cannot begin unless somebody takes on the role of Speaker, is an honour greater than any that has been conferred upon me at any time, and greater than anything my imagination could have conceived might happen to me in the future.

With the honour, of course, goes an obligation to do the job to the best of my ability, and, it goes without saying, to give it my best efforts at all times. At this moment I want to assure hon. members on both sides of the House, lest there be any doubt about it, that I place the fulfillment of this obligation ahead of every other consideration. Whether it be a question of party politics, personal considerations, friendships or otherwise, this obligation must at all times come first. I will fulfil the role as best I can. I will not always make everybody happy. However, if I can carry out this role to the best of my ability without losing the respect and the goodwill that you have extended to me at the start, because there could be no beginning without that, then I will finish the role a happier man than I began it.

Of course, it was appropriate for me to think in those terms because I made that speech from the Chair of the House of Commons in

Canada—which is not only a gift from the British Parliament at Westminster, but is an exact replica of the Speaker's Chair there.

There is, however, one notable exception—the Canadian Speaker's Chair has a seating plan taped to each arm, a difference far more substantial than any mere frill for the convenience of the Canadian Speaker. There could not be a seating plan taped to the original Chair because in the Chamber at Westminster there are no individual Members' desks—indeed there are no desks at all, only long benches. In fact, there are not even enough seats for all the Members. If you find that surprising, think of this: after the war damage to Westminster, the Chamber of the British House of Commons was rebuilt in exactly the same way. There are over 600 elected Members in the British Parliament, and seating for perhaps 400. Members, obviously, cannot rise in their place to make a speech; instead, they deliver it from a microphone on the Clerk's table or from a place of their choosing in the backbenches. This all stems from the basic concept of Parliament: that Members are not attached permanently to one side or the other, that they are expected to move about freely, and, having participated in debate and been persuaded by it, they will move to the side they favour. In Britain, that principle is carried further in the handling of recorded votes. Unlike Canada, voting cannot take place there by counting Members where they stand at their desk. The British Members divide and leave the Chamber through a door which designates whether they are voting for the "yeas" or "nays"—which is why the term "division" is interchangeable with the term "vote" in Parliament. The terminology has spilled over into the Canadian House of Commons, although the practice has not. It is also the reason why the bells which summon Members into the Chamber to vote in both places are called "division bells." Our Canadian Chamber (which, incidentally, is the only national legislature outside of Westminster to be known as the House of Commons) also has the Government and Opposition benches just slightly farther apart than the distance between two swords (could it really have originated in the hope that if worse came to worst, the swords wouldn't reach each other?), and in almost every other way bears great resemblance to Westminster. The Canadian practice of having individual Members' desks, which make the seating plan possible, is also related to the need in Canada for constant ongoing simultaneous translation—apparently impossible with any other arrangement.

These were not the only thoughts about this Parliamentary relationship going through my mind on that day. My head was filled with a whole range of questions which were not fully answered until quite some time later. I had been elected Speaker and yet the most visible aspect of my new responsibilities was that I would never speak in debate in the House. I was to preside over an assembly which opens with a speech from the Throne, delivered by the Governor-General, the Canadian representative of Her Majesty Queen Elizabeth II. The speech is written by neither of them, but by our Prime Minister. We are the elected Members of our national legislature, but before we may begin, we must go in procession to the Senate of Canada, where no one is elected. There we will learn from our Governor-General that Her Majesty wishes to inform us of her reason for summoning this Parliament, but will not do so until the Commoners have chosen a spokesman. It is only then that we return to our House of Commons to choose our representative—our Speaker. Can one observe such events, much less participate in them, without some reflection on how it all began and what it all means? Who is in control here? Is it our elected Members of Parliament and our Canadian Prime Minister, or is it the Queen, and is she really Queen of Canada?

I have no intention of turning this into a history lesson, but the answer can only be understood by looking back on the political conditions in England during the first ten centuries. In simple terms, the Monarch reigned with unrestrained power. Consultation, if it took place, was solely with those fortunate enough to form the Royal Court, a privileged retinue which owed its very existence to the pleasure of the Monarch. In certain respects, the British House of Lords, much as we know it today, evolved as the Court's formal or institutional structure. The rest of the population, the Commoners, were governed without voice, without involvement, until it was thought appropriate to turn to them for some of the cost of running the country. The cornerstone of what was to become the House of Commons was the principle that the Commoners must have their say in the affairs of the country if it was to be run with money extracted from them.

In covering ten centuries in five sentences, the over-simplification is obvious, but the fact is that these very same relationships and principles remain intact to this day. Members of the House of Commons still assemble to fulfil that most fundamental responsibility of holding the government accountable for the money it taxes from us in order to supply Her Majesty's needs in running the country. Were the Monarch to be present in Ottawa, it would be quite improper for her to pay a direct visit to the House of Commons where the Members insist on absolute freedom in such deliberations. Appropriately, she would appear in the Chamber of her own advisors, the Senate, and invite Members of the House of Commons there. Furthermore, the Members to this day still insist upon the right to have their grievances heard and redressed before approving such levies or expenditures.

Nor is it necessary to be a history buff to reflect upon the kind of reception given those first upstart assemblies by the King and his Court. Consider the poor devil chosen to preside over such early assemblies. He was the spokesman—Speaker—who had to convey to His Majesty those grievances to be resolved before the Commoners would agree to any levy to supply His Majesty's needs. Torture and imprisonment were commonplace in those days and more than one spokesman met violent death. The first of these, Sir John Bussy, served four consecutive Parliaments, but was beheaded without trial in 1399. The turning point is generally credited to the great Sir Thomas More who was Speaker over one hundred years later when Wolsey, as a messenger from Henry VIII, burst into the Commons to demand £800,000 for the war with France, to be raised by a tax of four shillings per pound on all land and chattels. The stony silence of the Members enraged Wolsey, but More's insistence that to return an answer without debate was "neither expedient nor agreeable with the ancient liberty of the House" sent him away. Lest we forget that hard won rights are easily lost, for more than a century even this fundamental freedom of debate remained in constant jeopardy. It fell then to William Lenthall, an otherwise unspectacular Speaker, to claim it for all time. On January 3, 1642, Charles I sent his Sergeant-at-Arms into the Commons to arrest five Members on suspicion of treason. They were in hiding, presumably with the help and support of their Commons colleagues. The next day, His Majesty strode into the Chamber, took over the Chair, and demanded delivery of the five. Unsuccessful, he pressed the Speaker to reveal their whereabouts, and Lenthall's response, upon his knees before the King, is engraved in Parliamentary history:

> May it please Your Majesty, I have neither eyes to see, nor tongue to speak in this place but as the House is pleased to direct me, whose servant I am here; and I humbly beg Your Majesty's pardon that I cannot give any other answer than this to what Your Majesty is pleased to demand of me.

We, of course, take it all for granted, but now and then it does no harm to reflect on the fact that it took over 300 years to achieve that much, and almost as long again to arrive at the level of Parliamentary sophistication which we inherited from the British at the time of Canadian Confederation in 1867. It is also part of that inheritance that the Queen of England is also our Queen, the Queen of Canada. She is Head of State here, as she is there. Title to all our state-owned land is in the name of the Crown as are prosecutions under our Criminal laws. Our duly enacted statutes only become law upon Royal Assent, and they bear the declaration:

> Her Majesty, by and with the advice and consent of the Senate and House of Commons of Canada, enacts as follows—

Perhaps most significantly, all money bills are entitled:

> An Act for Granting to Her Majesty certain sums of money for the Government of Canada for the financial year ending—

Her Majesty, upon advice from our Prime Minister, chooses a Governor-General to be her representative in Canada. And so it was entirely appropriate that, at the opening of Parliament in the afternoon of September 30, 1974, the Members of the House of Commons went together to the Senate so that I could deliver to the Governor-General, The Right Hon. Jules Léger, the same message that has always been delivered by the Speaker of the British House of Commons directly to Her Majesty at Westminster:

May it please Your Excellency, the House of Commons have elected me their Speaker though I am but little able to fulfill the important duties thus assigned to me. If in the performance of those duties I should at any time fall into error I pray that the fault may be imputed to me and not to the Commons whose servant I am and who through me the better to enable them to discharge their duty to their Queen and Country, humbly claim all their undoubted rights and privileges especially that they may have freedom of speech in their debates, access to Your Excellency's person at all reasonable times and that our proceedings may receive from Your Excellency the most favourable consideration.

Only upon receiving that assurance do we receive the Speech from the Throne. The nature of our reply will be the subject of the first major debate upon our return to our own Chamber. But before we turn to that most important topic, the Government will introduce a bill relating to Oaths of Office. The bill has absolutely no importance except to establish the right of the Commoners to set their own agenda even, and perhaps especially, when the business at hand is a response to an address from Her Majesty.

Now, of course, any real hostility in the relationship between the Monarch and her duly elected subjects disappeared long ago. In fact, there is in the Commons a highly visible symbol of Her Majesty's approval—the Mace. Originally intended to assist in protection of the King's person by the Sergeant-at-Arms, it is now bestowed as a gift to Parliament as a symbol of goodwill and, as a result, is given considerable prominence in House proceedings. In the Speaker's procession, which officially opens the daily sitting, the Mace is carried by the Sergeant-at-Arms. When the House is not in session, the Mace rests in a cabinet in the Speaker's private office. Following the fire in 1916, it was necessary for the House to resume sitting in temporary premises and a wooden replica of the Mace lost in the fire was crafted (until a new Mace could be properly made) so that it would be known that these temporary sittings were properly constituted and bore the approval of Her Majesty. That same wooden replica still stands in a cabinet in the Speaker's office, and I always asked the Sergeant-at-Arms to carry it into the House every year on the anniversary of the 1916 fire.

The present Mace was presented in May, 1916 to the Parliament of Canada by the Sheriffs of London to Prime Minister Borden at a ceremony in London, England. A portion of the previous Mace was recovered from the ashes of the 1916 fire, and incorporated into the new Mace. Once inside the Chamber, the Mace sits in a very prominent position on the Table of the House, and it is accepted among Members that the House is not properly in session without it. At times, business must be dealt with in the Committee of the Whole, so named, obviously, because it is a committee consisting of all Members of the House. The Chamber in these instances then becomes simply another committee meeting room, so the Speaker leaves the Chair and the meeting is presided over from the Clerk's chair at the head of the Table by the Deputy Speaker. The Mace is moved to a rack underneath the opposite end of the Table. The only time that the Mace is in the Chamber, but not in one of these two positions, is at the opening of Parliament when the House is summoned to elect a Speaker. Then and only then, it lies on a cushion on the floor.

I shouldn't leave the topic of the Mace without reference to what stands out in my mind as a very tangible illustration of the force of the concept. On June 1, 1956, the "Black Friday" of the famous Pipeline Debate, the House had been in unprecedented outrage and chaos, and finally was faced with the ultimate disgrace, the decision of Speaker Beaudoin, to turn the clock back 24 hours for the purpose of reconsidering his own decision. At that point, a number of very senior and very respected Opposition Members (their identities are not accurately recorded) attempted to take hold of the Mace and carry it out of the Chamber and thereby, in their minds at least, to end the legality of the proceedings of the House of Commons for that day.

But these relationships within our Parliamentary system cannot be understood solely on the basis of history. They must be grasped as concepts. Monarchy means more than the individual King or Queen: it is the concept of the truly benevolent Monarch, embodying everything virtuous in power or authority, which forms the cornerstone, or more appropriately the focal point, of Parliament. Parliament means more than one elected assembly: it is the concept of Parliament which embodies the best principles of freely elected democratic self-government. These institutions have endured because these concepts are timeless. Their interrelationships remain intact because they produce, in the Parliamentary system, a more responsive and responsible form of representative government than any other society has been able to discover. But it must also be understood that the relationship is not severable. Taking the Monarchy out of the Parliamentary system is like taking the nucleus out of an atom. Can we possibly conceive of any process by which some elected Canadian official, whom we might call a President instead of a Governor-General, might be entrusted by us with all of the power and authority that we now repose in the Monarch? The answer of course is that any such hybrid is most unlikely. It would be all but impossible to graft such a feature onto our Parliamentary system. If it were to be attempted, it would mean a total constitutional overhaul, contemplating all the same separation of powers and checks and balances between the President, Congress, Senate, and Judiciary that are the hallmarks of the American Congressional system.

So in the Parliamentary system we do not elect a President who is Head of State. We elect, indirectly, the primary advisor to the Queen—her First Minister. It is accepted that she will act only upon his advice only because he commands the confidence of the majority of the House of Commons. If a direct election were to produce a Prime Minister with no House of Commons majority, there would be no obligation upon the Queen to act upon his advice, and no certainty that the money to run the country would be supplied.

Above all, Parliament has endured because it works, particularly in terms of control. The Queen, who appears to have supreme authority, must act upon the advice of her Prime Minister. The Prime Minister, who also appears to have supreme authority, acquires that status only by commanding support of a majority of the Members of the House of Commons. Within the House of Commons, responsibility for directing the scrutiny of the actions of the Government falls to the leader of the majority Opposition party, who fulfills that function as a direct responsibility to the Monarch in the official capacity of Leader of Her Majesty's Loyal Opposition.

I have always been struck by the parallel with the adversarial approach in our courts, where the parties to a dispute put all the evidence and arguments in their favour through solicitors who have a primary responsibility to their clients, but who are also officers of the court. We accept the premise that, with all issues so fully and partisanly presented, the presiding judge or jury will then be able to arrive at the truth. In Parliament, the responsibility upon the Leader of Her Majesty's Loyal Opposition bears great similarity, and for that reason the office carries a personnel establishment and a range of services second only to those of the Prime Minister.

Furthermore, underlying all of this theory is a very specific and effective financial component. Her Majesty has no money to run the country except as supplied to her for that purpose by Parliament, upon the initiative of the elected House. And please, do not make the mistake of assuming that once a Parliamentary majority has been given to a party by the voters that a Prime Minister has *carte blanche* to ignore public opinion. The highest majority in Canadian history was obtained by The Right Hon. John Diefenbaker in 1958, with 206 seats of 264. Four years later, the voters reduced that to a minority, and then only a few months later, to a defeat. I was brought into the House of Commons during the "Trudeaumania" sweep of 1968, and exactly four years later, in 1972, The Hon. Robert Stanfield came within one or two seats of forming the Government. The 1974 Trudeau majority was lost to Prime Minister Clark in 1979, and six months later, the Clark Government was out of office.

Remember also the hazards of political leadership. In this huge, diversified country of ours, every region has different concerns. Policies that help industry hurt resources; what's good for fish is bad for lumber; please the farmer and antagonize the consumer; tackle inflation and increase unemployment. In addition, every time the Prime Minister recognizes one regional Member of Parliament with a Cabinet appointment, he disappoints ten others. It is just barely possible to keep everyone an enthusiastic supporter of the team if you continue to win. If the party loses, it is all but impossible.

Finally, no one is better at anticipating the changes in the mood of voters than the elected Members—after all, their very livelihood depends on it. Long before the voters in 1962 took away the huge Diefenbaker majority, his own caucus had begun to turn, not just to resistance, but to palace revolt. Surely the 1974 Trudeau government went five years before calling the 1979 election because the political experts and the Liberal caucus knew that defeat was coming. Loss of faith at that time by as few as a dozen back-benchers would have been critical. Consider then the tremor in the Liberal Government ranks in 1983 when a letter was signed by almost twice that number of Government Members, including more than one Cabinet Minister, calling for a reconsideration of portions of the MacEachen budget—about as close as you can come to a public declaration of lack of confidence in your own Government. The cold reality is that political leaders can never take their own elected supporters for granted, much less the voters.

Appropriately then, the controlling factor in the Parliamentary formula is in the hands of the electorate. The Queen's power as Head of State is limited by her obligation to act only upon the advice of her Prime Minister. He remains Prime Minister only so long as he commands the support of a majority of the House of Commons, the elected body which retains final authority over any money supplied to the Queen. The initial majority can only be obtained from the electorate, and can only be sustained by a successful, popular leader with a commendable legislative pro-gramme and policies for which he and his Cabinet are constantly accountable to Parliament.

Above all other considerations, it is the Speaker's solemn obli-gation to ensure that Parliament functions fully and effectively in that regard. My first act was to assure the House of protection from outside interference, including the Sovereign, in perform-ing these duties. I very quickly learned that from then on most of my time would be spent protecting Members from each other—or in more Parliamentary terms, safeguarding and balancing the rights of all Members. It proved to be the most singular, demand-ing, yet satisfying challenge I ever expect to meet.

The official duties went on most of the rest of that first day. They began with a reception for all of the Members and guests, and all official guests at the opening of Parliament, including the entire Diplomatic Corps. Barry and I stood by the table in the middle of the beautiful Speaker's chambers and the guests were brought through in a receiving line that, as I recall, lasted the better part of two hours. It was our introduction to hosting those gatherings of a few thousand people which only seem to occur in the nation's capital. Later that evening, we entertained our own personal guests at dinner in the large private dining-room on the north side of the Speaker's corridor—set aside for formal dinners hosted by the Speaker. Right next door, in the north-west corner of the main floor, there is a small apartment which I occupied during the entire first session.

It was Barry's preference to have Megan born in Sudbury (November 28 of that year) so we didn't move down to Ottawa as a family until the beginning of the session after the first summer recess, but we did all come down to Kingsmere for Christmas break. The Gatineau Hills are beautiful in the fall, but Kingsmere and the surrounding grounds seem to be even more spectacular in mid-winter. We had some friends in to stay with us. During the day, we skied at Camp Fortune and came back to have a drink or two in front of the fire and then enjoyed an after-dinner stroll. The finest evening of all was when we serenaded the few neighbours close by with some Christmas carols. During the rest of the winter, I continued to commute to Sudbury on the weekends, as I had done every weekend during all of the years I was a Member. The next fall, September of 1975, we all moved in together. That was the year of our delegation to the Soviet Union, and we barely had enough time to move in when I was on my way overseas. We have a special memento to mark the initiation of Kingsmere as a family residence. Barry accompanied me to the airport, and we left the three boys in charge of Megan—with a strict admonition of course that they stay right by her side at every moment. Need I tell you that before we were around the first corner, they decided that this would be a perfect occasion to take their first drive around the neighbourhood, the oldest being 12! To their abject terror, they didn't get any further than the gate at the front of the huge circular driveway where they managed to slide one wheel into the gatepost!

The drive down from Kingsmere through the Gatineau Hills is beautiful at any time of year, and it certainly was a perfect way for me to start the day. I would usually arrive at the Speaker's private entrance on the west side of the Centre Block and begin the day by looking through the morning papers during breakfast in the small dining-room. If there were no emergencies, (which was about half the time), the rest of the morning would be spent in any one of a number of ways. Two mornings a week, I took French lessons under the tutelage of Madame Claudette Chemla of the House of Commons Language School, whose expert needling and prodding was really responsible for whatever mastery I now have of the French language. Quite often there would be a couple of hours on an open-line radio programme by conference call to Sudbury. If not, it gave me a chance to spend some time with the staff on correspondence and constituency problems.

Quite frequently, there would be a session, usually a little over an hour in length, with a number of groups that I was anxious to encourage. These included service clubs, adventure in Citizenship programmes, career development programmes among public servants, and study groups from the private sector. One of these, Forum for Young Canadians, for example, was a programme under which a young man from Western Canada named Joe Clark made his first appearance in the House of Commons. During all of my years, one of the staff organisers of the programme was Mr. Barry Turner of Ottawa, now the Member for Ottawa-Carleton. These sessions usually involved an appearance in the Chamber, or perhaps in a conference room, but in every case it was something I would gladly have done all day long. The interchange with Canadians at all levels who expressed this kind of interest in our proceedings was not only a pleasure, but surely must be looked upon by all of us as an investment in Canada's future.

By 11 o'clock, it would be time for our daily meeting of Table Officers. The Clerk and all of his senior staff, the Deputy Speaker and his assistants, and I would gather to anticipate any problems that might arise during the afternoon session. In later years, I reduced the frequency of these meetings to two or three a week, but always on the understanding that in special circumstances, we would all be available. Almost invariably, there was some official entertaining to do at lunch, anything from a meeting of the Commissioners of Internal Economy, Management Members' Services Committee, Restaurant Committee, Press Gallery Executive, or various incoming delegations. During lunch, notices would arrive of any Members seeking an emergency debate and lunch would be interrupted for a brief discussion with the Clerks about the proper ruling.

By about 1:45 p.m., it was time to change into the Speaker's robes. A few minutes before 2 o'clock, we would line up in the Speaker's procession, which included the Sergeant-at-Arms carrying the Mace, the Clerk, a page carrying the prayer card, and myself. We would begin promptly at 2 o'clock and proceed along the Speaker's corridor to the Hall of Honour, the Centre Block's main corridor, then along the south corridor into the main entrance of the Chamber. We would say prayers (alternating French and English each day), then the doors would open to let in the public and the members of the Press Gallery, and we would go on to the opening of the session and Question Period. I was always required to stay in the Chair after Question Period in order to go through the introduction of the remaining routine business and to resolve any procedural disputes. That would absorb anywhere from half an hour to two hours. When finished, I would give the Chair over to the Deputy Speaker and return to the Speaker's chambers. The ensuing few minutes were reserved daily for any Members who wanted to come in to chat about their difficulty in getting recognized on that day.

In the first year, I found that many times, especially if Question Period or the argument following had been particularly intense, I needed to get out of the building for a few minutes and walk around on the grounds overlooking the Ottawa River. Private Members' hour began at 5 o'clock and if there was no procedural debate, I knew I wouldn't be required back in the Chamber at least until 8 o'clock and usually quite a bit later. If there was no official dinner, which occurred once or twice a week, I would have the driver take me up to Kingsmere to have dinner with the family. About half the time, I would have to come back down to Ottawa around 9 o'clock, either to settle a procedural point or because of a recorded vote, so the day would finish at 10:30 in the evening—long enough indeed, but most of it quite pleasant. Question Period and the beginning of each session involved a lot of high pressure, but by and large, the rest of the time was spent with some very interesting people in a most convivial atmosphere.

3. Question Period

If the essence of Parliament is Government accountability, then surely the essence of accountability is the Question Period in the Canadian House of Commons. And make no mistake – in Canada it is accountability to a level unmatched in any elected assembly in the world.

In the great Mother of Parliaments, British Ministers, including the Prime Minister, are not in the House unless they have been put on notice. In the American Congressional system, the President appears at a time and on subjects of his choice – before the press. He is never questioned by his political foes in either the House or the Senate.

The Canadian Prime Minister and his entire cabinet are, without advance warning, subject to daily examination by their political rivals. And now the televising of Canadian Parliamentary proceedings adds the ultimate degree of the most important single element of democratic self-government – public participation. This puts Canada in the forefront among the nations of the world in holding those in power accountable to their electors. It also happens to make fairly good television viewing, probably because it is always topical, fast-moving and instantly comprehensible to the viewer (unlike a good deal of the rest of the legislative proceedings).

It simply is not possible to prepare anyone to preside over Question Period. I have been blessed with a pretty good memory for names and even now, any time I am together with former Members from the early years, I can still quite easily call them not only by their first and last family name, but in nine cases out of ten, by the name of their constituency. When I took the Chair in

1974, I probably could have done it with half the Opposition and likely two out of three members in the Government backbench, so I took considerable comfort in knowing that it would take me at least a couple of weeks to go through my own personal supply of familiar faces—by which time I was fairly sure I could get to know all the rest in the same way. To a very great extent, that's exactly how it turned out. Even so, my first sight of 75 M.P.'s springing to their feet as each question was dealt with was colossally unnerving, particularly on the second day when I blissfully assumed that the 20 who had been up on the first day would be good enough to sit it out to give their colleagues a chance. Quite the reverse—they were twice as keen, and they were spurred on by the idea that since they had apparently found the magic formula for getting recognized on the first day, their chances were better than anybody else from then on. My self-assurance quickly turned to dread of reflexively reverting to that handful of Members I knew and allowing them up on consecutive days, while 40 or 50 of their colleagues might go unrecognized.

This may be an appropriate place to clarify the subject of proper designations for Members of the House of Commons. An elected Member is never referred to in the House by name, always by constituency, and always as "The Honourable Member for—e.g.—Sudbury." This, of course, is a recognition that all Members acquire standing in the House of Commons in precisely the same way: at the hands of their own electorate. Members never address each other directly, but always address their remarks to the Chair. Even in putting questions to Ministers during Question Period, it is in such terms as "Mr. Speaker, my question is for The Right Honourable the Prime Minister. Would the Prime Minister inform the House, etc." Members are always referred to as "Honourable Members" in discussions in the House, but that does not carry into the designation of "Honourable" outside the House. In Canada we reserve that designation for Members of Her Majesty's Privy Council. It is, of course, for Her Majesty to choose Privy Councillors as she pleases, but in doing so she acts, as she must always do, upon the advice of her Prime Minister. It is also axiomatic that the Cabinet, the executive branch of government in the Canadian Parliamentary system, is the active committee of the Privy Council and therefore all Cabinet Ministers are sworn into the Privy Council. It is also a Canadian practice to admit both Speakers and Opposition Party Leaders to Privy Council membership, but not usually until their retirement. One Minister of the Crown is designated as the President of the Privy Council and almost invariably combines that responsibility with the role of Government House Leader. Cabinet is served by a secretariat called the Privy Council Office and the Clerk of the Privy Council is the senior and most powerful member of the Public Service. The head of the Cabinet team, of course, is the Prime Minister who alone carries the designation "The Right Honourable." At any time, the Speaker is properly referred to as either "Mr. Speaker" or "Your Honour." Customarily, Canadian Cabinet Ministers use the title Honourable only during their active years, but continue for life to place the initials P.C. after their names. Not to be confused with the Conservative Party, the initials stand for Privy Council.

There is a printed seating plan taped to the arm of the Speaker's Chair. This is simply a reprint of the floor plan from the pamphlet handed out to visitors, Opposition side on the left and Government on the right, but as soon as we were under way, it became obvious that it wasn't going to be of much help. You can just imagine the scene—the entire House is kept waiting in embarrassed silence while I scan 150 squares on the Opposition seating plan trying to locate the Member who wants to be recognized—especially during the rapid-fire exchange of Question Period when everything runs at a split-second pace. It could hardly be much worse were I to simply ask the unknown Member to introduce himself!

I began to keep my own lists. The first year I kept a handwritten list for Question Period which I would begin to prepare as soon as I recognized the lead-off speaker. Just before Question Period, each party's Whip would designate the identity of their lead-off speaker. In the case of the Conservatives, it would usually be the Leader of the Opposition, followed by one of his front-bench Members pursuing the same subject. It was understood that they would have two questioners before we went to the first N.D.P. Member, again usually the Party Leader. In my first years, the same process was then followed with respect to the Social Credit Party, although, because of their smaller numbers, not every day.

All of this gave me about ten minutes to identify other Members who were trying to get recognized and to jot down some names; but 25 participants was maximum, and with the inevitable long questions, long answers, accusations of stalling on the Government's part, or of impropriety on the part of the questioner, it was often closer to 15. With 50 to 60 people on their feet, including some on the pre-determined list and about a dozen slots open, it quickly become a painful reality that for every person recognized, literally ten would go away frustrated every day.

Originally, this "oral" Question Period grew out of the Members' rights to put written questions to the Government of the day, a right which still exists and is very widely used. Initially, from time to time, the Government would be pressed to give oral answers to those written questions which required an urgent response, and this gradually evolved into a daily agenda item. As a result, and sad to say (as is so often the case in practices of this sort) the first time I consulted the respected authorities on Parliamentary procedure for Question Period, I was saddened to see a litany of prohibition. The only guidance was from precedents ruling questions out of order. After I had had a few months to feel comfortable with Question Period, I looked for the right opportunity to attempt to express my view of its governing principles in positive rather than negative terms. The occasion was just after the House initiated, on an experimental basis, a very important change in practice.

When I began in 1974, any Member who felt aggrieved or dissatisfied with the ministerial approach or lack of it on any given issue would raise a point of order or a question of privilege which had to be dealt with immediately. The Speaker was expected in some way to keep track of the time used for these procedural interruptions and attempt to adjust the duration of the Question Period accordingly. It was an unhappy practice in every way and I was most delighted when the House agreed on what quickly became a permanent change: that of leaving any procedural matters until the conclusion of Question Period. As a result, Question Period now begins at 2:15 and ends at three o'clock, when the procedural points can be dealt with in a far more orderly fashion.

This is the text of my statement concerning Question Period to the House on April 14, 1975:

On Monday last, the House began an experiment with a change in procedure relating to the question period, Standing Order 43, supply and ministerial statements. I indicated earlier that I would make a statement today in respect of the changes. This statement concerns itself with the question period only and as I indicated before the Easter break ought to be taken as a reference point for discussion and consideration by Members before the Standing Committee on Procedure and Organization, where I will be happy to appear if Members wish. It is therefore not so much a decision as it is an explanation of my understanding of how our question period should operate. The question period is a unique feature of the Canadian House of Commons where the ministry is required to be accountable to the House on a daily basis without advance notice. It is an excellent feature of our Parliament and while we have much to learn from other governmental systems, the question period is one area in which we are in the forefront of responsible government and every effort must be made to preserve the excellence of this practice.

The opportunity of Members to put questions has developed in a rather haphazard way, but it is now enshrined in Standing Order 39 and if it ever was considered to be a privilege of Members it certainly now enjoys the status of a right. Much has been said in the precedents about restrictions and disqualifications or interferences with the right of Members to put questions. This is not the approach I prefer to take in attempting to establish a rational approach and understanding concerning how the question period should operate. I much prefer to take the positive approach of attempting to arrive at a statement of principle within which questions can be put and to reduce to an absolute minimum the negative disqualifications that may limit or restrict a Member's right so to do. In so doing, I should say that there seems to be no question that the Speaker enjoys discretion in allowing a question and certainly in allowing a supplementary. I think it is also important to begin with the rather wide latitude of discretion that is given the Ministers to whom questions are put.

The fact is that Ministers are able to make an answer of

course. They may also defer a question for further consideration or take it as notice. Ministers are able to make an explanation if for some reason they are unable to make an answer at that moment, or finally, they may say nothing. It therefore seems to me that any basic principle governing the question period ought to be such that it will enable Members to put questions with a minimum of interference. In examining the many precedents, I feel that principle can best be stated as follows: A brief question seeking information about an important matter of some urgency which falls within the administrative responsibility of the government or of the specific Minister to whom it is addressed is in order. This statement bears some explanation. First, it must be a question. That seems to be too self-evident to be worth consideration. However, the fact of the matter is that that statement is put right at the beginning because it opposes such things as expressions of opinion, representations, argumentation or debate.

Second, the question must be brief. There can be no doubt that the greatest enemy of the question period is the Member who offends this most important principle. In putting the original question on any subject a Member may require an explanatory remark but there is no reason for such a preamble to exceed one carefully drawn sentence. It is my proposal to ask all honourable Members to pay close attention to this admonition and to bring them to order if they fail to do so. It bears repeating that the long preamble or long question takes an unfair share of the time and invariably in provoking the same kind of response, only compounds the difficulty. Replies ought to be subject precisely to the same admonition. On the subject of supplementaries, I again suggest to Honourable Members the adoption of a practice which recently was suggested by one of our provincial colleagues which is—if and when supplementary questions are allowed there ought to be no need whatsoever for any preamble.

The supplementary question is a follow-up device flowing from the response and ought to be a precise question put directly and immediately to the Minister, without any further statement. Third, the question ought to seek information and therefore cannot be based upon a hypothesis, cannot seek an opinion either legal or otherwise and must not suggest its own answer, be argumentative or make a representation. Fourth, it ought to be on an important matter which again is self-evident but it is stressed here again in order to rule out frivolous questions. Fifth, the matter ought to be of some urgency. This is not included to intend in any way to be similar to those questions of urgency which are included within the Standing Orders surrounding special debates. It is here only to stress the fact that there must be some present value in seeking the information during the question period as opposed to seeking it through the Order Paper or through correspondence with the Minister or the department.

The fact that questions on the Order Paper also have been changed in the experimental order to daily responses, I am sure, is to all honourable Members an indication of the goodwill and good intentions of the government in making more prompt answers to the questions on the Order Paper. If the government will do so, undoubtedly this will have a beneficial effect on the conduct of the oral question period. At the same time, it goes without saying that the vexatious or frivolous use of the right of putting questions on the Order Paper by putting questions which do not seek the kind of information which can be available within a reasonable time and reasonable effort and expense seems to me to be only a waste of the time of the House and to invite the government to use the excuse that it would take too long or cost too much money to make replies. In other words, a serious and conscientious attitude on both sides about the use of the Order Paper for information will certainly go a long way toward improving the oral question period.

Sixth, a question must be within the administrative responsibility of the government or the Minister. Obviously, the government in general cannot be responsible for those areas which are beyond its own administrative responsibility. Furthermore, the Minister to whom the question is directed is liable to the House, responsible to the House, for his ministry, that is his present ministry. He is responsible to the limits of that ministry but not beyond that. In this regard, I find no reason to change the earlier decision I made in respect of the capacities ministers enjoyed previously in other portfolios.

It seems to me that a question which conforms with this basic principle ought not to be interfered with without a clear reason. One or two are well known. Obviously, the question must adhere to the proprieties of the House in respect of inferences, imputing motives, or casting aspersions upon persons within the House or out of it for that matter, but this is no more a rule of decorum in the question period than it is out of it. The same rules surround polite language and things of that nature.

There is a clear precedent that if a question has previously been answered it ought not to be asked again. A question cannot deal with a matter that is before a court. Those are clear restrictions. There are three others which seems to me lend themselves to some confusion. Perhaps I may be able to clarify this, but I am not sure. The first deals with statements made by Ministers outside the House. This, it seems to me, is a matter of form rather than one of substance, for indeed if a question otherwise conforms with the principle I have set out then it ought not to be disqualified simply because in its preamble some reference is made to a Minister or a statement made by a Minister some place other than here. For the life of me, I cannot undertand why, in the case of a valid question, a Member would want to tie it to a statement made outside the House and therefore risk having it disqualified when, in fact, the simple device is to put the question directly without any reference to the statement.

There have been restrictions related to questions about government policy. It seems to me that a question which seeks opinion about government policy probably is out of order because it seeks an opinion rather than information. A question which seeks a general statement of government policy may be out of order because it requires the kind of long answer that ought to be given on statements during motions or in debate. But this is the kind of qualification which is referred to in the statement of principle. Otherwise, it seems to me that every question that is asked and answered and which has been held in order for as long as the question period goes back has in one way or another a connection with government policy.

The third area of confusion is in respect of anticipating orders of the day. It is a restriction that is not well understood. If I might express it in my own terms it simply means that if the subject of debate for today concerns, for example, housing policy, then questions on housing policy ought not to be taken during the question period.

That, simply, it seems to me, has obvious reference to the currency or importance of the question being taken at that time rather than at some other time. Similarly if a special debate has been ordered for later in the day because obviously the topic is very important and very topical the proper course would be for the Chair to defer questions until that debate is on rather than permit them during the question period.

Beyond that I think a word should be said about points of order and questions of privilege. One of the most significant features of our experimental order is the suggestion to the Chair that points of order and questions of privilege be deferred until three o'clock. I say this is most significant because it is obviously an expression of the consensus of honourable Members that those who prolong their share of the question period by arguing points of order and questions of privilege are really doing nothing more than extending the time that has already been granted to them to put questions. There is no need for a full exposé of questions of privilege and points of order. Suffice it to say that for the purpose of the question period that all honourable Members know, and know well, that complaints about the failure of a Minister to give an answer about the quality of the answer that any Minister has given, or about discrepancies in answers given by different Ministers or by the same Minister on different occasions may be valid comments for debate at the appropriate time but do not, by any stretch of the rules, constitute a question of privilege or a point of order.

Even in handling these matters when they are deferred until three o'clock, it seems to me to be in the best interests of the House—unless a Member is able to establish at the beginning when addressing himself to these points that he has some point of order or question of privilege that has some basis in procedure other than a mere complaint of that sort—to discourage Members from raising such complaints at the start.

Finally, I should like to add in respect of honourable Members' rights about questions which they feel have not been adequately dealt with during the question period that there is provision for an adjournment debate. Consideration may be given by the committee to expanding that—certainly it has been recently considered. In any case, it is an excellent way for Members who feel that the answer has been too brief or that they have not had the opportunity to fully develop a question to seek to raise it again in the late show.

After six sitting days under the experimental order, there can be no doubt that it has been successful, but in my view, the success is attributable, as it always is, not so much to the rules themselves or to the power or discretion of the Chair but rather to the attitude of Members of the House.

It is not possible to say too much about the importance of this because when Members in their questions and Ministers in their replies choose to abide by these principles that I have tried to set out here, the question period runs smoothly with a maximum participation. On the other hand, when Members or Ministers choose to disregard these principles, they can be called to order by the Chair, but that question period cannot be saved from the damage that has been done to it. In the first six days, it is obvious that Members have looked upon this experiment with a positive and conscientious attitude, which, if it continues, will assure that this very worthwhile experiment will become a permanent Standing Order. My authority is simply an expression of the desire of Members that the proceedings run well and have maximum value. But, I am sure Members understand very clearly that the less the Chair is called upon to interfere in the proceedings, the better.

With further experience, it became evident that even the small number of restrictions which I dealt with could be reduced. Perhaps more significantly, I realized that even in cases where the proposed question would seem to run afoul of the rules, it was better for all sides to leave the appropriate objection to the Minister rather than do it myself. When done by the Speaker, it has the appearance of shielding the Government, which no one wants—least of all the Minister to whom the question is directed. Bear in mind that no rule compels the Minister to answer, so the response—including the lack of it—is entirely the choice of that Minister on that day. The final sanction is public opinion about the individual Minister or the Government.

It is the right of the Speaker alone, of course, to determine who shall have the floor, but at all times during debate that practice is governed very extensively by consultation between the party Whips, House Leaders, and the Chair, so that a rotation is maintained in balance and Members in each party can plan their participation in advance. Although I always looked on party involvement in the House as a help rather than a hindrance, the same kind of input to Question Period is not nearly as simple. It has always been an accepted practice for all parties to indicate their lead-off questioners. Frequently, I also welcomed their input with respect to any backbench Members who were under special pressure on a particular topic which I would naturally be unaware of. At first, it was confined to the first two Conservatives who would be taken together before the N.D.P. Leader. After a few weeks, the Chief Opposition Whip, Mr. Paproski (Edmonton-Centre), asked if he could carry it a step further and identify the second-round questioner (after the other Party Leaders) in the same way. I was glad to accede because, almost as much as the lead-off questioners for each party, this is a focal point for any pre-planned strategy, since it opens up the series of questions which follow possibly for the rest of that day. Failure to recognize their designated Member at this point could de-rail a strategy involving the next five or six questions and, in my view, there was no need for me to set aside such strategy lightly, so long as it didn't unfairly squeeze out their backbench.

By contrast, the N.D.P. approach was very much a full caucus effort. After their daily strategy meeting, their Whip or House Leader would give me three names—the maximum possible. Almost without exception, I followed their suggested list, and had virtually no complaint from their membership. Indeed, I never had any difficulty about party strategy in Question Period at all—even in 1979 when we went to the other extreme. In Opposition (most of them for the first time after more than ten years in power), the Liberals tried several approaches and, before two weeks had gone by, designated a former Minister, The Hon. Pierre DeBané (Matane) to take charge. He asked if we could try a suggested list for the entire time. I gave it a good deal of thought, found no great objection in principle, and agreed to experiment until Christmas. I joked that if he was anxious to absorb the daily wrath of his disappointed colleagues, it would be the least I could do to accommodate him. Before we had a chance to benefit from the experiment, the House dissolved that December, with the defeat of the Clark Government.

But nothing could ever totally eliminate the enormous frustration: every day, two or three Members would come to see me after Question Period (I always kept that part of the daily schedule open). Some were new M.P.s, anxious to make a mark, some were very senior, even with special "shadow-cabinet" responsibilities. Always their agony—and it was genuine—was the same: not one but two, and sometimes three consecutive attempts to put a question would be to no avail. And this might be occasionally accentuated by their being recognized only to find that the Minister in question was missing for that day—or even just for those few minutes when they had the floor.

From the start, I kept cumulative lists of Members missed during Question Period—in fact I couldn't hope to do it myself, so I had one of the Table Officers watch carefully and compile it as soon as he could. The idea was to give priority during the last few minutes to any Members who had been passed over one or two days earlier. It didn't solve the problem entirely, but Members were always pleasantly surprised to learn of the extent of the effort made on their behalf—and also to know that I wasn't ignoring them on purpose (or that I just couldn't see!). I guess there was never a day that I didn't yearn for the sort of "Speaker's Dream Question Period" when everyone kept at it until every last question had been dealt with.

One of the most delicate problems is the supplementary question. Party Leaders were routinely entitled to an opening question and two supplementaries. Properly used, there is hope of a progression—first, to set the scene; second, to set the Minister up; third, to deliver the knock-out punch. Naturally, every Member wants the same chance, but I was constantly fighting the clock

−crowding long preambles or long answers−trying to hold other Members to two and sometimes one question. I never really made any permanent headway, and I doubt any Speaker ever will because it treads upon deeply felt emotions about equal treatment for every Member. Let me illustrate: very early in the first year, I recognized the Conservative critic on Regional Development, Mr. David MacDonald (Egmont). We went through a rather long first question and answer, and a similar supplementary. We were more than half-way through the alloted time and there was the usual relentless pressure from other Members. When I didn't allow him a second supplementary, he blurted out that I had done it to protect the Government−likely the most offensive remark imaginable about a Speaker! It was all the more astonishing knowing him. David MacDonald is a United Church Minister. He appropriately took a balanced, intelligent, and compassionate stance in debate, regardless of the issue−so I couldn't believe my ears. But then transfer payments and regional disparity were close to his heart−especially as a Maritimer. He had prepared his sequence of questions and had set up his target, like every other front-bench critic, only to have it taken away from him because I had focused entirely on the time factor and on the unceasing pressure to keep things moving. In any case, after I had caught my breath, I said I hadn't heard him (although he was no more than ten feet away), and that perhaps we'd both be helped if he could step out of the Chamber long enough to let it pass−which he did−and, more typically, returned a bit later to apologize.

An offshoot of Question Period that wasn't very much in public view served as one of the most meaningful practices for Members on both sides of the House. It was affectionately dubbed "The Late Show" because it began at 10 o'clock each evening when the House normally adjourned. The practice was to consider that the Standing Order for adjournment was actually debatable for 30 minutes during which an expanded version of three questions could be put and answered. The questions had to originate from the Question Period of an earlier day in respect to which the Member was dissatisfied with the answer given. When the Member so advised the Table Officers, the question was automatically added to the "Late Show" list. Each day at 5 o'clock, the three questions selected for later that evening would be announced from the Chair and, when called at 10 o'clock, the questioner was permitted three minutes and the replier, usually a Parliamentary Secretary, was expected to use seven minutes for an obviously far more comprehensive reply than would be permitted during the Question Period. It was, and in my opinion always will be, precisely the kind of vehicle that best serves conscientious Members either in Opposition or in Government. Its best feature is that it allows for direct confrontation and obviously meaningful response on any grievance that is under some time pressure.

I can't leave the subject of Question Period without telling you a couple of interesting side events. For the first, I must introduce Mr. Léo Robitaille—the Chief Steward. I was his fifth Speaker and as this book goes to press, he has gone on to service with Mme Jeanne Sauvé, Lloyd Francis, and John Bosley, which brings him some 30 years in the service of Parliament, beginning as a busboy in the Parliamentary restaurant. He is in every sense a "Man Friday." Whether taking charge as the Maitre d' whenever I hosted an official dinner, perhaps for the Prime Minister, the Governor-General, or some visiting delegation from assemblies around the world, or whether he was simply making sure that I had a clean shirt or didn't lose my luggage, he was, without question, absolutely indispensable. Each day, the Sergeant-at-Arms, the Clerk, Table Officers, and the Speaker form a procession through the Hall of Honour and down the south corridor into the main entrance of the Chamber to signal the start of the sitting. Léo immediately noticed that I had reading glasses in my jacket pocket which I couldn't carry dressed in the Speaker's regalia, and he offered to polish them and to place them on the arm of the Speaker's Chair while we were in the procession.

On my second day, when I got into the Chair and looked to my right, I cannot remember looking at a more forlorn human being than Léo, cradling my broken glasses in his hands. I couldn't read my list, the floor plan, or anything else without them, so the only answer was to borrow a pair from the nearest Member—who unfortunately had a head the size of a football. I couldn't help but laugh to myself all during Question Period at what must have looked like something out of vaudeville, as I tried to get accustomed to the strange surroundings, gathering my funny looking garb around me, and trying to hold on to the over-sized pair of pince-nez reading glasses. Léo and I often shared some

1. The Jerome family photo for the 1968 campaign. From left to right: Mary Lou, Barry, Joe, Paul, the author, Jim Jr., and the family dog, Doctor.

2. The Jerome family portrait for their 1979 Christmas card, in the living-room at Kingsmere. Left to right, back row: the author, Paul, Mary Lou. Left to right, front row: Joey, Barry, with Megan on her knee, and Jim Jr.

3

4

5

3. James Jerome is "dragged" to the Chair for the first time on September 30, 1974.

4. A view of Speaker's corridor, which runs along the north end of the House of Commons, with the portraits of Canadian Speakers since pre-Confederation lining the walls.

5. The Speaker's procession precedes the daily opening of each session in the House. The Sergeant-at-Arms, Colonel D. C. Currie, carries the Mace. Speaker James Jerome follows behind.

6. Speaker James Jerome presides over prayers, held before the opening of Parliament each day, and attended by Members of the House, as well as the Clerks, Table Officers, and pages, shown here. Clerk of the House of Commons, Beverley Koester, stands slightly to the right of the Chair, just in front of the Table.

7. Sergeant-at-Arms Major-General G. M. Cloutier places the Mace on the Table of the House.

8. On the occasion of the 100th anniversary of the Parliamentary Library, this cake was fashioned as an exact replica of the Library building.

9

10

11

9. In September, 1977, the Chamber of the House of Commons underwent drastic alteration in order to accommodate the new "electronic Hansard": television.

10. Four weeks later, on October 16, 1977, the Chamber was back to normal, and the first televised session went without a hitch.

11. Speaker James Jerome and part of the first page group, which he was instrumental in introducing to the House, in 1978.

12. James Jerome is sworn in as an elected MP for the third time in 1979. With him are most of the Ottawa staff who worked together during the events in this book. Left to right: Barry, Léo Robitaille, Georgie Bracken, Ron Dalpé, Anna Favretto (La Ballister), Edna Clifford, Carmen Dumont, Suzanne Nicholas, Kim O'Neil, Alister Fraser.

13. At the Sudbury testimonial dinner for James Jerome, the crowd sings "Happy Birthday" to Stanley Knowles. From left to right: Walter Baker, P.C., Knowles, Judy Erola, P.C., Archbishop Alexander Carter, diocese of Sault Ste. Marie, and Walter Curlook, executive vice-president of Inco Ltd.

14. Former Speaker James Jerome's portrait is unveiled in 1980 in Speaker's Corridor, and presided over by his successor, Speaker Mme. Jeanne Sauvé.

15. The author shares a light moment with the Right Honourable Member for Prince Albert, Mr. Diefenbaker, as he welcomes him for a celebration of the former prime minister's 75th birthday.

16

17

16. In the Speaker's chambers: an early 1975 visit from U.S. Secretary of the Treasury, William McNamara, with his host and Canadian counterpart, Hon. John Turner, then Minister of Finance. From left to right: Alister Fraser, John Turner, an unidentified assistant to McNamara, Mrs. Turner, William McNamara, and James Jerome.

17. Speaker James Jerome escorts Her Majesty Queen Elizabeth II during her visit to Canada in 1978 on the occasion of the 25th anniversary of her coronation.

18. Governor-General Jules Léger is presented with the scroll carrying the inscribed House resolutions in reply to the Speech from the Throne by Speaker James Jerome at Government House during the winter of 1975. Left to right: Mme. Léger, Léger, Jerome, and Senate Speaker Lapointe; Steve Paproski (Edmonton-Centre) is in the background.

18

19

20

19. An official state visit by French Prime Minister Raymond Barre. From left to right: Speaker Lapointe, Barre, former Prime Minister Trudeau, Jerome, and Deputy-Speaker Gérald Laniel.

20. Speaker Jerome's last official delegation outside Canada: Premier Hua Guofeng, in China, January, 1979. From left to right: James Jerome, Guofeng, Senator Lapointe, and in the background, Allan MacEachen, P.C., and Mrs. Joan André (wife of Harvey André, Calgary Centre, not in this picture).

21. Speaker Jerome receives a medal from Xavier Deneux on behalf of l'Association Internationale des Parlementaires de Langue Française as a tribute to having become a bilingual Member of the House of Commons.

21

22. Speaker James Jerome presides from the Chair.

good times about that story, especially his relief when he found out the hard way whether his fifth Speaker had a sense of humour.

Let me also introduce Mr. Sam Macrillo, who has been the masseur to Members of Parliament almost the same length of time. When I was first elected in '68, I used to drop down to his shop directly beneath the House of Commons Chamber in the Centre Block for a steam bath and quick rub-down. I never dreamt that one of the hazards of assuming the Speaker's Chair would put me back in Sam's hands for emergency treatment! For the first several weeks as Speaker, I was suffering a pain in my back for the first time in my life. Finally one morning, when I almost had to get help to get out of the car, Léo took me right to Sam. He had no trouble locating the problem—it was a very big and very tight muscular knot on the upper left side of my back. Sam worked it out and said he was sure that after two or three days, he would have it in shape. When I returned a second time, he said he couldn't help wondering about it the night before, and so he had slipped into the gallery during Question Period just to confirm his suspicions. Sure enough, as soon as Question Period began, I huddled against the left arm of the Chair and didn't move until Question Period was over. That is of course where the Opposition floor plan is located. As soon as I took his advice and made sure I kept moving around on that huge throne, the problem disappeared!

It seems appropriate to close on Question Period with a special reference to a special person—The Right Honourable Member for Prince Albert, John Diefenbaker. The character of our relationship during his last years was really struck on my first day in the Chair. We were past the half-way point and it was "so far so good" (too early for things to go sour). I had given the floor to Mr. Mazankowski (Vegreville). Remember that with every question, 40 or 50 Members rise to seek the floor, and each time the Speaker designates someone, everyone else starts to sit down while the lucky Member does a quick reverse as his recognition from the Chair penetrates—and quickly rises to put his question. In this case, Mr. Mazankowski was rising, but so was Mr. Diefenbaker, who had the seat right in front of him. As the two of them stood, the Chamber grew quiet and Diefenbaker spoke: "Mr. Speaker, I have been trying to get recognized to put a question."

The silence became deafening and, after a pause that seemed to me to be endless, I said: "Order please, The Hon. Member for Vegreville." The whole House knew that I had already given him the floor, but as soon as he finished his supplementary question, I immediately gave the floor to Mr. Diefenbaker.

Later in the day, Mr. Diefenbaker spoke in the Throne Speech debate and, although I was never required to stay in the Chair during all speeches, I made a point of staying in during all of his and always did thereafter out of respect for him as a former Prime Minister. During the course of his remarks, he paid me quite a compliment. He referred back to an exchange we had had when I first spoke in the procedural debate in 1968. He felt then that I had a promising future in Parliament and was good enough to say so. He also said that he felt certain that my performance, even in the brief period up to that point, demonstrated that I would likely be a fair, objective and impartial Speaker. It was quite obviously more than the customary complimentary remark that everyone extends to a new Speaker, and I believe he meant it. At that point, it was also a pat on the back that I very much needed.

In the five years that followed, until his death, it was transparent that he was the beneficiary of special treatment as far as I was concerned. It was obvious that he could not go through the rigours of hopping up and down like a new Member and so, either through his party Whip or through a seat-mate, he would give me an indication of any Question Period in which he wanted to participate. In this way, I was able to recognize him on virtually every occasion he wanted, and I never had the impression that he sought the floor more often than he should have. However, during Question Period, he often went on longer than I would have normally permitted any other Member, but none of his caucus ever complained and I was always very careful to make sure that his time wasn't at the expense of the other Opposition parties.

But if I create the impression that John Diefenbaker had somehow been purified in his later years, let me quickly disabuse you of that notion. I could always tell when he was going to tread on the rules. Instead of facing the Chair, he would look down toward the other end of the Chamber, while he reached in his desk for newspaper clippings or some other prop to mount an attack or to otherwise enrage the Government Members. At times, he wasn't above a convenient hearing difficulty if I attempted to interrupt him from over his shoulder. When I first arrived in Parliament, we tangled briefly in debate and I would not have known that my participation had won his respect unless he had been kind enough to say so in public. In his later years, he mellowed into a great Canadian statesman and it was this John Diefenbaker that I came to know.

I remember particularly one instance in late 1977. I had made a ruling which did not concern him directly but which he misunderstood on the basis of a word which he thought I had used and which had not appeared in Hansard. As a result, he said at the time that he felt the ruling was wrong and that he would seek the appropriate opportunity to raise it in the House. Several days went by as he did some research on it and during that time his long-time aide Keith Martin and Alistair Fraser, the Clerk of the House of Commons, had some discussions about it. It had the potential of blowing into quite a serious matter and they were pleased to be able to arrange a private meeting between us before he raised it in the House. When he arrived in the office, he outlined his version of the matter and I was quickly able to point out to him that he had simply heard a word that I had not used. When he was shown the word that I did use, the matter was over. He then sat and chatted for almost two full hours. Suddenly there was no Parliamentary crisis here—this was simply a great veteran of Parliament looking for some company. When I had arrived as a hot-shot new Member in 1968, ready to take on the world, John Diefenbaker was the highest profile in the enemy ranks, and in my maiden speech I went right after him. In 1979, when his funeral train pulled out of the Ottawa station, I was on it!

Of course, all exchanges during Question Period were not so easily resolved. Within a few days, it became obvious that Government backbenchers were unhappy about their share of time. I would recognize at least one and sometimes as many as three of them, but never with supplementaries for obvious reasons. The essence of Question Period is accountability, and no one could ever persuade me that Ministers were really under critical scrutiny from their own Government supporters.

But an even more acute situation was building up with respect to Parliamentary Secretaries. Having been one and having answered questions in the House for my own and sometimes for other Ministers, it never occurred to me that Parliamentary Secretaries should also enjoy the right to ask questions. Although several of them were on their feet in the first few days, I deliberately passed them by. So it was in week five, when after several unsuccessful attempts at recognition, Mr. Joseph Guay (Saint-Boniface), Parliamentary Secretary to the Minister of Regional Economic Expansion, rose on a question of privilege:

> If a Parliamentary Secretary is not to be recognized in the House for the purpose of asking a question—and the people of his constituency expect him to rise in the House once in a while and ask questions—I believe, sir, that you ought to tell the House that you will not recognize us.

My ruling was quick and unequivocal:

> Indeed, I welcome this question of privilege for that very purpose. I have, of course, to consider whether some Members of the House are eligible to use the time of the question period to pose questions to the ministry. It is obvious, certainly, that members of the ministry ought not to enjoy the privilege of being able to both represent the Government in answering questions in the House of Commons and, in turn, to use the time of the Question Period to ask questions.
>
> Similarly, the privilege, of course, of being elevated to the position of Parliamentary Secretary falls only on those among the Government ranks. This extends to those Hon. Members, not only the recognition, prestige and advantage that comes from their position but the obligation of answering questions, because not only do they occasionally answer questions during the question period, but they do so on a regular basis during the "late show" proceedings at 10 p.m. when they answer for the ministry. I have taken the position, to which I hold, that those who are clothed with the responsibility of answering for the Government ought not to use the time of the question period for the privilege of asking questions of the Government.

I had, of course, given the matter a good deal of thought. What I had failed to do was to give anyone an opportunity to argue! Immediately, both The Hon. Mitchell Sharp, Government House

Leader, and The Hon. John Turner, Minister of Finance, jumped up to seek at least a later discussion where I might hear all Members affected. My reaction only made it worse. I indicated that having given my reasons, I would be pleased to listen to any view or representations to the contrary. Both Opposition House Leaders, Conservative Gerald Baldwin and N.D.P. Stanley Knowles, together with the Right Honourable John Diefenbaker, roared into the fray and they were on firm ground. Whether I had allowed arguments or not, and whether the Government liked it or not, I had made a ruling and it had to stand. Whether I wanted it or not, further discussion could only be characterized as an affront to me, or as an appeal from my ruling, which is directly prohibited by Standing Order 12. It took a while for the storm to subside, but let me assure you it was the last time I got discussion and decision in reverse order.

4. Games Members Play

As you might expect, the main event in Parliament centres around "Government Business," which covers the entire programme put forward by the Government of the day. The majority of House rules and the greater part of the timetable are given over to it. It is also the major preoccupation of the political parties, and demands a very high level of discipline not only among Government supporters, but in the orchestration of the Opposition attack as well. Whether on a general policy statement in the Throne Speech, a general financial statement in the budget, or on any aspect of the legislative programme, each party must act as a team.

The public and the media love to see a maverick on the scene now and then, but over the long haul virtually every elected Member is very closely identified with the party platform. The fact is that voters tend to be suspicious of Members who can't get along with their own party (just check the track record of those who have bolted party ranks to seek election as independent candidates). The individual Member's input and impact is far more likely to take place within caucus than it is in the final discussions in the House itself. Within caucus the objective is modification of the party position so that, even though less than perfect for each Member, it at least becomes worthy of their public support. Occasionally, Members find party discipline stifling, and they become disillusioned with the extent to which they have to sacrifice the chance for personal impact in the interests of the greater goal of party popularity. But that is simply the way party politics is, and the individual Member on both sides of the House can very easily be swallowed up in the process. The ideal, of course, is for the Member to support the party in major policy positions and yet still be able to break loose often enough to shine as an individual.

All of this produces two events which unfold at the same time, one political and one personal. Both provide more than their share of fireworks and are aspects of Parliament that have always held special fascination for me. The political ingredient springs from the Opposition's drive to convince the voters they made a mistake in electing the current Government, and to demonstrate why they should reverse that result at the next opportunity. The personal one springs from the efforts of the individual Member to be seen as a faithful party Member and a good constituency M.P., but also as an individual rising star. Whatever strategy may be employed, the initial objective is to divert Parliament's attention from Government business. If that can be done, the ultimate accomplishment is to force Parliament to a decision favourable to the Opposition. The first is extremely difficult, the second almost impossible. It takes ingenuity, imagination, and above all persistence, but, as I hope to demonstrate in these following pages, it can be done—sometimes very effectively. If in the process Members have to be reminded of the rules, their dexterity can be dazzling. It is attributed to a mischievous Irishman to have said:

Mr. Speaker, I know you would find it to be a very grave question of privilege were I to describe my Liberal opponents as sewer rats, but I can't help wondering if we were a Parliament of sewer rats, would it be a question of privilege to call one of them a Liberal?

There is no shortage of opportunity to speak out on major issues, particularly along the general party line. Each session of Parliament begins with eight days of "Throne Speech Debate": appropriately, a very general discussion on the entire range of Government policy. There is usually a similar six-day budget debate and, of course, extensive consideration of every Government bill. When you add in the 25 days in which the Opposition has the right to designate the subject for debate, the problem is not a lack of opportunity to get off a speech on the national or international issues. It is when the matter is urgent, short range, or of local concern that the array of procedural weapons is greatly reduced.

Question Period, of course, is the number one weapon, but the time constraints are obvious. With a duration of 45 minutes, and at least half of the time given over to lead-off questions by Party Leaders or other front-bench critics, there are realistically a maximum of ten openings for backbench Members in any given day. The mathematical chance of being recognized on the right day with the right Minister in the House is so small that even the most ingenious Member cannot survive on Question Period alone. There is an interesting parallel here with the Private Member's hour, a special time set aside two or three days a week devoted to private Members' attempts to pass bills, to debate motions, or to compel the Government to surrender documents. The time available is so small in relation to the number of Members seeking access that many give up on the idea. Those few who prevail against the very long odds often come away frustrated because the Government has found it necessary to send in one or two Parliamentary Secretaries to make sure that the debate lasts the entire hour without a decision.

When these avenues fail, the Member turns to a number of procedural devices that I want to deal with at some length. They used to include daily applications for the unanimous consent of the House which, of course, will permit any Member to introduce a motion without notice. There are similar specific rules permitting applications for emergency debates. Failing these, the two favourites are the question of privilege and the point of order. Both are very strictly defined. The question of privilege is limited to remarks or conduct showing contempt for Parliament, or, in the case of an individual Member, conduct which prevents the Member from carrying out his duties to the House. The point of order is limited to drawing the attention of the Chair to a breach of House rules or practices which must be corrected before business can proceed. In actual fact, they are used daily, particularly following Question Period, and quite often are intended to do nothing more than express dissatisfaction with ministerial response that day. When that was the case, there was no question of privilege or point of order, but there was no way that I could make that determination until I had heard the Member's opening remarks. Often as not, that was all the Member ever hoped to accomplish. A great many others, of course, were quite serious and were the subject of carefully prepared procedural presentations absorbing several hours of debate and requiring a reserved decision on my part.

During the preparation of this book, I was pleased to learn that the Clerk of the House of Commons, Dr. Beverley Koester, had launched a project to compile, edit, and publish selected decisions of Canadian Speakers. As a matter of convenience, the first part of the project covers my term, and was prepared under the direction of Mrs. Mary Anne Griffiths, Clerk Assistant (Research) for release in 1982. After eliminating those decisions set aside in routine fashion, the researchers were still left with over 300 for more detailed review and over 100 for publication. It is a much higher number than I would have expected, so I have had to be even more selective in the number I want to share with you. Some posed relatively minor problems for me, but made headlines, others attracted very little attention, but had potentially dire consequences.

Lest I create the impression that Parliamentary gamesmanship plays a pre-eminent role in the House, let me begin with a reference to one very important incident for me. It should also serve as an illustration of a very important fact of life in Parliament. When the seriousness of the situation demands it, and particularly when Parliament or the Speakership are under attack, individual and party differences are quickly set aside in favour of a consensus to express the collective opinion of the House. Ironically, the event in question was a non-decision not directly related to Members of the House of Commons at all.

Motion of Censure—*The Globe and Mail*
After the summer recess in 1976, when the House resumed on October 12, some employees of Canadian Press, who were then members of the Parliamentary Press Gallery, were on a rotating strike. Canadian Press is a newswire service owned cooperatively by Canadian newspaper companies. As an employer, it sought to replace the striking employees with other jounalists, who would have required temporary memberships in the Parliamentary Press Gallery. Since the Gallery's function is to report Parliament to the Canadian people, it is a responsibility of Parliament, and

therefore of the Speaker, to ensure that it is able to do so properly. All of the day-to-day operation, including rules and regulations covering accreditation of new Press Gallery members, has always been left to the elected executive, but there is no doubt that the Speaker always has ultimate authority to intervene if there is any breakdown in the function of reporting Parliament to the public. In this case, the Gallery gave the applications for temporary membership formal consideration and rejected them. Canadian Press, by letter dated November 26th, asked me to intervene.

In my view, however, there was no indication either from Members or from the media of any deterioration in the reporting of Parliament, and, therefore, no need for me to take exceptional measures. In addition, of course, this was not a work stoppage of the whole of the Parliamentary Gallery, but rather an individual labour dispute by employees of the Canadian Press, one of several services represented in Gallery membership. I therefore declined to intervene and left the matter to be resolved between the parties.

There were persuasive arguments on both sides of this issue, and the debate in the newspapers was very extensive. Then, on December 22, 1976, the following editorial appeared in *The Globe and Mail:*

CENSOR IN THE COMMONS

Speaker James Jerome of the House of Commons has rejected freedom of the press, freedom of communication between Canadians, and he has done it with the assistance of newspapermen who are members of the Parliamentary Press Gallery.

During the recent rotating strikes of employees of The Canadian Press, press gallery members voted to withhold temporary gallery accreditation to CP employees whom they deemed to be strike-breakers. The Canadian Press appealed to the Speaker, who must take responsibility for excluding any person from the press gallery of the Commons. Mr. Jerome has written Canadian Press rejecting its claim that its parliamentary operations were subjected to censorship during the labor dispute. He has approved the exclusions imposed on behalf of the union.

Strangely, he convicts himself of censorship with his own pen. "The press gallery function," he wrote, "is more than a commercial news reporting service. It is an integral part of our work; a service which Parliament must safeguard for the Canadian public who are entitled as a right to the fullest information on activities here." Yet he threw away that right of the Canadian public to take, instead, the side of a union in a labour dispute.

The commercial element which he mentions has no place in the House of Commons. Press people are entirely entitled to strike their companies, to strike associations of their companies. But neither they nor their companies should be permitted to carry the dispute into the press gallery which belongs not to them but to the people of Canada. They are no more than pipelines from Parliament to the people, and when they block those pipelines, allow them only to be used by persons of whom they approve—when the Speaker permits them to do it—they censor what is delivered to the people.

They have set a precedent which ought to terrify them. It took centuries to compel Parliament to conduct the people's business in public, in front of people who would report what it had done. For a long time the cry of "I spy a stranger" permitted members of Parliament to dismiss news people from the House, and do in secrecy what they feared the public, if it knew about it, would not approve.

Now the newsmen, the pipelines themselves, have been permitted to spy the strangers and push them out, for their own commercial purposes. The next time the precedent could be turned against themselves, or against any reporter whom they or the politicians wish to exclude.

It is a dreadful backward step, for it puts in place the machinery for delivering to the people only what a combine of Parliament and the press believes should be delivered. It jeopardizes the right to report on Parliament by unpopular messengers who very frequently, in the world's history, have been the only messengers to carry the truth. It is censorship to curry favor with the unions; and fewer than a third of Canada's workers are union members.

The Speaker–James Jerome–has failed the nation in the Parliamentary Press Gallery. There is only one way, now, to correct the error. Television and radio are to be admitted to cover the House. The people themselves must also be admitted. The silly rule, which forbids any citizen who is in a public gallery and not the press gallery to make notes, should be ended.

Any Canadian should be able, from now on, to sit in the public gallery and take down what the elected say and do. He should always have been able to do so. Now it may be the only way of ensuring that all the facts are made available to the public. Let it be said of James Jerome that he is not a speaker but a gambler who plays incredible odds for the popularity of his party.

When I read it, I was as much puzzled as I was insulted. The editorial conveniently left out any reference to the fact that the management of *The Globe and Mail* shared responsibility for the operation of the Canadian Press service, so they were clearly in a management position in this dispute. The idea of any element of censorship is really stretching things incredibly, but the suggestion (happily, the only one–ever) that I was somehow playing "incredible odds for the popularity of his party" was senseless, and more important, clearly contemptuous. Inside the House of Commons, no elected Member would ever be permitted to even come close to such an attack on the Speaker's integrity, but this was outside the House and in a newspaper editorial. I knew I couldn't simply let it pass, but I wasn't quite sure about what to do. I gave some thought to an immediate discussion with House Leaders, but I am delighted to say that they didn't have to wait for an invitation from me. When the House met at 2 p.m., it gave unanimous approval to a motion proposed by The Hon. Allan MacEachen, President of the Privy Council, and Government House Leader:

That the statement "Let it be said of James Jerome that he is not a Speaker but a gambler who plays incredible odds for the popularity of his party" contained in the editorial in *The Globe and Mail* on December 22, 1976, is a gross libel on Mr.

Speaker, and that the publication of the article is a gross breach of the privileges of this House.

It was an emotional moment for me and I thanked all Members for such an immediate and forceful gesture of support.

Unparliamentary Language

Unparliamentary language is always a thorny problem (the one that I least enjoyed), arising only when emotions are running high and the mood of the House gets very ugly. Insults are always distasteful and very awkward for any Speaker, especially when they draw the national political leaders into personal animosity. Adjudication is made all the more difficult because in theory it should be possible to say almost anything in Parliament. The restriction is on the *way* it is said. It is obviously acceptable for a Member to say black is black and to say that the Minister says black is white, and thus let the House and the public judge upon the truthfulness of the Minister. It is unacceptable, however, to call the Minister a liar, a coward, or to accuse any Member of deliberately misleading the House. Nor are the precedents in this matter of much use: depending on the context, the same expression may have been rejected by one Speaker and accepted by another. This middle ground often gave rise to what I felt was petty bickering – prolonged by a sort of whining complaint that the original offending language had not been clearly and unequivocally withdrawn. In doing research for this book, I was pleased to find that a good many of these incidents looked every bit as silly in Hansard as they seemed at the time.

Three were very serious indeed – two leading to expulsion of a Member from the Chamber, a third to the brink of real crisis. The first happened on May 16, 1978, and it was obviously very dramatic for me. Mr. Roch LaSalle (Joliette), during Question Period, plainly and simply called the Minister of Finance, (The Hon. Jean Chrétien) a liar. The Chrétien budget contained very controversial proposals to withdraw from certain areas of taxation and to compensate the provinces accordingly. The moment the proposals were released, the Minister was under attack for violating the sacred principle of budget secrecy on the premise that the compensation must be negotiated in advance with the provinces. Just as the attack was dying down, Quebec took the position that it had never approved this before and wouldn't accept it now. Mr. LaSalle knew this was suddenly the best and most publicized issue to come his way in all his years in Parliament, and he pressed the attack at every turn. On May 16, during the preamble to his question, I thought I heard him use the term "liar," but he was speaking very quickly in French, so I wasn't sure. I asked him to put his question immediately and when he did, he removed any uncertainty:

> Mr. Speaker, here is my question. The Minister of Finance intended this as a direct incentive to industry. Yesterday, he recognized that his formula was not a direct incentive. So, I conclude that he deliberately lied to Canadian people, and I ask him to apologize to them.

The Minister rose on a question of privilege and I knew the dreaded moment had arrived. At least one thing was clear, the expression "liar" is not subject to dispute. And after I asked him to withdraw, Mr. LaSalle quickly made it clear as well that his use of it was not accidental:

> Mr. Speaker, if I understood well, you want me to withdraw. In view of the commitments made by the Minister regarding the proposals contained in his budget, and after what he did, I repeat that he is a liar.

I asked him two more times with the same result. Some of the Members sought a brief recess, or an opportunity to discuss the point, but there could be no doubt. I "named" him (it is the only occasion when a Member is called by name rather than "The Honourable Member for Joliette"). Contrary to popular view, however, the Speaker cannot discipline the offending Member. That must be done by the House upon motion for that purpose, customarily proposed by the Government House Leader. I quote Mr. MacEachen's remarks in full, because while they resolved this problem, they also held grave overtones for the crisis of June 30, 1978:

> Mr. Speaker, because of the importance of the situation that has arisen I feel I should explain, at least to the satisfaction of myself, the proceeding in which I am now engaged.

It has been the tradition of the House of Commons that when the Speaker names any particular member, the leader of the government in the House supports the Speaker in that decision. That, I believe, has been the unvarying tradition of the House of Commons with one exception, and when that occurred the Speaker of the day was left in a very exposed, unprotected, and unsupported position. It is therefore my desire in discharging my responsibility to support the Speaker.

I would add that while the Speaker did make the suggestion that I put this motion, it is a decision which the leader of the government in the House makes on his own account, and he can either agree—or disagree to move the motion. With that in mind, Mr. Speaker, and in accordance with the responsibility that you must discharge to the House, and in support of your responsibility, I would move, seconded by the Minister of Justice (Mr. Basford):

> That the hon. member for Joliette be suspended from the service of the House for the remainder of this day's sitting.

The motion carried and Mr. LaSalle obediently left the Chamber for the rest of the day.

The second instance involving an Opposition Member and unparliamentary language was on March 21, 1979. The late Mr. Tom Cossitt (Leeds) accused the Prime Minister of deliberately misleading the House. The Hansard record reports the essential portion of it as follows:

Mr. Cossitt: On the question of privilege raised by the hon. member for Battle River (Mr. Malone) a moment ago, the parliamentary secretary, referring to certain questions I had asked, made what from his point of view was a value judgment that my questions were stupid and unreasonable. I feel it is an infringement on the privileges of members of this House that one man sitting over there should have the right to say who he thinks is stupid over here and who he thinks is unreasonable, and edit the answers to questions accordingly. If that is what the government is doing in dealing with these questions, I think it is a shocking admission and a breach of privilege.

In answer to one specific question, the Prime Minister (Mr. Trudeau) intentionally misled the House a few moments ago: he said a question had been answered, when he knows it has not.

Mr. Speaker: I think the hon. member for Leeds would prefer that I did not hear the last remark he made. If I did, as he knows, I will have to ask him to withdraw it.

Then I have to say we cannot allow our proceedings to continue with that remark on the record. The allegation that a Member has intentionally misled the House is unparliamentary and I must ask the hon. member for Leeds to withdraw that statement.

Mr. Cossitt: I would certainly be prepared to withdraw it provided the Prime Minister is prepared to say it was unintentional. Otherwise, I cannot withdraw it.

Mr. Speaker: Order. The hon. member has made a statement which is clearly unparliamentary. Such a statement is clearly unparliamentary according to precedent. The statement to which I refer is the statement by the hon. member for Leeds that the Prime Minister intentionally misled the House. Now, the House cannot continue with that statement on the record. The hon. member has to withdraw it.

An hon. Member: Withdraw or get out!

Mr. Speaker: Order, please. Once again, before invoking a practice which I would follow only with deep regret, I have to tell the hon. member for Leeds for the third time that he has introduced into the record an expression which is clearly and unequivocally unparliamentary. The allegation by one member against another that he intentionally misled the House is clearly unparliamentary. The House cannot proceed in the face of that kind of disorder and I have to ask the hon. member for Leeds to respect the practices of the House and withdraw that expression.

Mr. Cossitt: I regret very much that I believe what I said and I cannot speak any untruth.

Some hon. Members: Shame!

Mr. Speaker: With the greatest regret, therefore, I have to name Mr. Cossitt for his disregard of the directives and the authority of the Chair.

In due course, the appropriate motion suspending The Hon. Member for Leeds from duties in the House of Commons for the balance of the day was carried, and Mr. Cossitt left the Chamber.

The most critical incident during my tenure involving unparliamentary language happened on June 30, 1978. It was a dramatic one for Parliament, indeed for the country. In fact, it led to this newspaper headline in early July:

NOW IT CAN BE TOLD!
PARLIAMENT, ON JUNE 30, TEETERED ON THE BRINK OF COLLAPSE, DISSOLUTION, AND A GENERAL ELECTION.

It began quite innocently during Question Period on Thursday, June 29, 1978, when Mr. Elmer MacKay (Central Nova) put what seemed to be a routine question to the Minister of State for Urban Affairs (The Hon. André Ouellet), related to a Robert Campeau building project in Hull. The Minister's reply was equally unremarkable, until he used these words:

> It seems obvious to me that the hon. member, as always, is trying to discover scandals where none exist and allows himself, as he has done in the past, to continue to sling mud in the face of French Canadians.

At the end of Question Period, Mr. MacKay rose on a question of privilege:

> If I understand the record correctly, I rise on what I consider to be a despicable attempt to impute motives, made by the Minister of State of Urban Affairs (Mr. Ouellet), that I am somehow adverse to the interests of Canadians of French descent.

He was supported by others, including N.D.P. Leader Ed Broadbent:

> For me this is a very serious matter, particularly at this stage in the history of our country. In terms of matters of privilege,

to call someone a racist, because that is what is involved, is just every bit as offensive as calling someone a liar in the House of Commons.

He was also supported by the Conservative House Leader, the late Hon. Walter Baker:

Mr. Speaker, the acts of the minister and the words of the minister have been described as despicable. They could be described as being beneath contempt, they could be described as being vicious and vulgar, and they could be described in a lot of ways—

This was the fourth year of the Parliament, which almost always brings about an election. Rumours to that effect had been rampant for six months. But only days earlier, it had become quite definite that it would not take place in the summer, and that the session would carry on into the fall. None of this did anything to improve the atmosphere in the House which was already quite testy. The only slight consolation was that the House Leaders had reached an understanding that we would break for two months at the close of business on Friday, June 30. Under House rules at that time, this kind of prolonged adjournment required a special motion which could only be introduced with unanimous consent. As an indication of how fragile these "understandings" can be, in my 13 years as a Member we only failed to sit in July of 1974 and 1979 when we had summer elections. So no one had any illusions about the tendency of this pact to self-destruct—and what better detonator than a bitter French-English donnybrook. I, for one, was prepared to do what I could to avoid it. I did not guess that I would put Parliament and myself in jeopardy in the process.

Although the previous day I had assured the House of an opportunity to argue Mr. MacKay's question of privilege (which would normally follow Question Period) I had an inspiration as I took the Chair on that Friday. I thought that it was perhaps only a one-day issue that everyone would prefer to set aside quickly. Acting on impulse, I put the suggestion to the Minister before calling oral questions:

Having regard to the words which were spoken by the minister yesterday—of course, in the heat of the exchange—I cannot come to any other conclusion than that the words had, as their effect, an imputation of motives of the hon. member for Central Nova and that in his questions about Les Terrasses de la Chaudière he was aiming some criticism at a group of Canadians of French origin. I, therefore, feel that in the heat of the moment the minister overstepped the line and was out of order in making that imputation against the hon. member for Central Nova, and I am sure that the minister would want, before proceeding further with the question period this morning, to withdraw that allegation.

It was a very grave miscalculation! The Minister was more than happy to defend his record over any suggestion of favoured treatment for any French-Canadian. So were a number of his colleagues who had prepared supporting submissions. Furthermore, the procedural issue was far from clear, and Allan Mac-Eachen, as Government House Leader, had come prepared to lead the argument that the Minister's words had broken neither rule nor precedent, and therefore he could not be required to withdraw. Cabinet solidarity would demand the Government House Leader to support a Member of his own Cabinet team, so there certainly would be no motion put by the Government House Leader if the Minister refused to obey a directive from the Chair. Such a motion would undoubtedly be put by an Opposition Member, but without doubt would be defeated by the Government majority. I would have had then no choice but to accept that as an expression of lack of confidence in the Speaker.

On a momentary impulse, I had quickly painted myself into a corner from which there could very well be only one exit—my resignation. In the Minister's initial response, he indicated that he was ready to debate the issue, and I again asked him to withdraw. This is the full text of the rest of the exchange:

Mr. Ouellet: Mr. Speaker, you are asking me to say that the hon. member did not want to attack French Canadians and to withdraw my remarks. I am prepared to do it, but I submit to the House that the hon. member questions the actions of people, whatever their origin may be, be it Polish or Lithuanian or whatever. Their origin has no importance whatsoever. Of course, the fact that in reading again the hon.

member's numerous interventions in Hansard in recent months —

Mr. Speaker: Order, please. I want to remind the minister that yesterday, when argument was made on this question of privilege, he was in the House and did not take that occasion to argue the merits of the case. Now that the Chair has made a ruling on the language and on the arguments that were made yesterday, it is no longer open to debate or discussion. It seems to me that the minister must either obey the direction of the Chair to withdraw the offending remark and allow us to get on to other business, or presumably some other course will have to be taken. The minister has said to me that he is ready to withdraw the remark: that is different from withdrawing it. I want the remark withdrawn before we proceed with any other business.

Mr. Ouellet: Mr. Speaker, if it is only accidentally that the hon. member asks questions about people such as Gauthier, Perrier, Marchand, Lapointe, Giguère, Pratte, Ménard, Campeau, Joanisse —

Mr. Speaker: Order, please. I will see the minister one more time to withdraw his remark, as the Chair has directed, and permit us to go on to other business. Otherwise, I have to follow another course.

Mr. Ouellet: Mr. Speaker, if it is true that the hon. member did so accidentally, then I of course withdraw my remarks because he is the most inconsequential and petty individual this Parliament has ever known. It is without realizing it that the hon. member discredits and casts doubt on French Canadians. So I am forced to withdraw my remarks but I think he is a petty individual whose actions are dangerous.

As you can see, it was something less than an unqualified retraction, but it met the technical requirements and allowed us to move on to Question Period. We did rise later that day for the promised summer break which, happily, gave Honourable Members, the press, and me, more pleasant things to occupy our attention.

Was the newspaper headline accurate in its reference to a risk of dissolution of Parliament and a general election? I'm afraid so.

Quite clearly, without the Speaker, the House cannot meet. In the atmosphere of that moment, it is not difficult to imagine the hostility engendered among Opposition parties at a Government which would sacrifice the Speaker on this kind of issue. What would their attitude have been toward any nomination from the Government ranks for a new Speaker? Indeed, would any Member have accepted a new nomination if the entire procedure were resisted by all Opposition Members?

Are there alternatives? That is very difficult to answer. Because of the dire consequences, I could have exercised the rare prerogative of adjourning the House at the Speaker's initiative for the purpose of discussing the situation with the House Leaders, but the problem was not and is not unique. Usually, when unparliamentary language occurs, it is used by Opposition members in attacks upon a Minister. The ultimate motion of censure to support the Speaker is therefore forthcoming as a matter of course and is supported by the Government majority. But where the offending Member is also a member of the Cabinet, the formula breaks down completely and the matter becomes a confrontation between the Minister and the Speaker in which only the Speaker stands to lose. The complications were greatly intensified in this instance because the Minister's response did not fall into that category of clearly unequivocal unparliamentary expressions. I wish there were easy conclusions, but there are none. The same situation can occur any day in any Parliament and create the same crisis.

Worst Decision

There is an expression among lawyers: bad cases make bad law. When a compassionate judge tries to write a judgment in favour of someone who really should lose, what really suffers is the quality of the law. That certainly applies to what I consider to be my worst decision. It sprang from one of the results of the 1979 election: the reduction of the Social Credit Party ranks to five. Party status in the House carries a number of very important benefits. Each Party Leader, House Leader, and Whip are recognized officially by the House, and have extra allowances, space, staff, and other facilities for that purpose. In addition, during the 29th Parliament (1972-74) funds for research staff were allocated in proportion to House representation. In order to be eligible, a party had to have 12 seats.

In 1974, when it appeared that the Social Credit Party might fall below that number, the House agreed, as a courtesy to a long-time and beloved veteran, Mr. Réal Caouette (Temiscamingue), to continue to treat him as a Party Leader as long as he remained in the House. In fact, after his death, we continued to extend the same courtesy to his successor. But in 1979, with only five Social Credit seats, everyone knew the end had come. That didn't make the transition any less awkward however, certainly not for me. To begin with I had to be the final arbiter of disputes over seating. There were serious arguments about whether the Social Credit Party was entitled to sit as a group, and if so, whether they should occupy any front row seats—which has always been looked upon as a badge of party status. I gave them the benefit of the doubt on both counts and allocated a bank of seats at the far end of the Chamber on the same side as the Government, including a front row seat for their Party Leader. That issue was barely settled when the next one arose, and it was not under my control.

At the beginning of every Parliament, a Striking Committee is established for the purpose of channelling the nominations from each party caucus for membership on the various standing committees of the House. The membership for the Striking Committee is chosen so as to reflect the membership in the House itself, but more importantly, it consists of the House Leaders or Whips of every party—the ones responsible for seeing to it that Members are up to the mark in every aspect of House duty. The contents of the motion to establish the standing committees are always negotiated in advance by the House Leaders, and the motion is passed with a routine voice vote. In this case, because of the touchy situation about Social Credit membership, the motion had to be introduced formally and was the subject of brief debate and a recorded vote. In the event, the vote rejected the proposed inclusion of a Social Credit Member on the Striking Committee and was therefore a clear and formal indication of the total rejection by the House of the party status of the Social Credit.

Awkward or not, it was at least an official decision of the House, as opposed to any area in which I might enjoy personal discretion. I should have had the good sense to simply follow that principle on a strict basis. Instead, I attempted to soften the blow by extending some special courteous treatment to the Social Credit group. It seemed a simple enough thing to do at the start, but before we had finished with it, it blew into a very dark storm indeed.

In every session there are 25 days set aside to debate subjects posed by the Opposition. On November 7, the Leader of the Opposition (Mr. Trudeau) used one of the days allocated for Opposition debate to move a motion of non-confidence in the Clark Government. In such debates, since they stem from an Opposition motion, it is customary to recognize all Opposition Party Leaders before giving the floor to the first Government Member (usually a Minister). I took that occasion to suggest to the House that, although the Social Credit did not enjoy party status, since they were going to have one speaker in the debate anyway (although normally quite a bit later in the day), I would, as a courtesy, call upon their acting leader, Mr. Fabien Roy (Beauce) in the rotation normally reserved for leaders.

Hansard contains this record:

Mr. Speaker: Order. I see three members seeking the floor and, of course, it is my responsibility to choose. Since the first day of this session, I have attempted to reconcile in my own mind events that have taken place and which, I am sure, have not escaped the attention of the members of this House. They relate to the position of the members of the Social Credit party in the House.

We ought to be clear at the outset that it is not a transgression of propriety to mention the name of the political party or the members who are involved; it is the Social Credit Party of Canada. Its members are members of this House of Commons and their leader is the hon. member for Beauce (Mr. Roy). Those are the realities.

What the House dealt with on opening day, as is its long-standing practice, was a motion which related to membership on a striking committee. . . .

I want to go back to that and stress again to the House that that vote, even indicating, as it did, that the House was reacting or expressing itself on the position in which a member or members of a party holding five seats finds itself in the House of Commons, I think we ought to be clear that that is the status: we have a political party with a leader and with five members in the House of Commons. The vote under no circumstances, may I say, can be taken to pass out of existence a political party, nor can it be taken to render as independent members the group which has been recognized as a party and which has, in fact, been seated together as a political party. The Social Credit Party of Canada exists as a political party and the five members exist as members of that party under their leader.

Faced with the decision by the House on the one hand, which was, in my opinion, an expression of what the entitlement of that group then becomes, the House decided at that time that that group, as a political party in the House, was not entitled to membership automatically on the striking committee. The House is entitled to make those expressions because the House has to decide whether a party of five members is entitled to the same things as a party of 26 members or a party of 112 members. Those are decisions that the House has to make. The House, in my opinion, made a declaration to that effect on that day, and I have said so several times. I have no intention of retreating from that position.

On the other hand, it seems to me that the responsibility of the Chair and the responsibility of the House of Commons is to protect whatever rights minorities do enjoy and, therefore, it seems to me that I must conclude what it is that the members of the Social Credit party are entitled to. For example, as I have said, participation in the question period is their right, the same as any other group of five members. It is not difficult to calculate mathematically what five members are entitled to as a proportion of the 26 members and a proportion in terms of the 112 members that sit opposite them. Therefore, I come to the conclusion that the members of that party are entitled to a certain participation.

The House will recognize in what I have tried to do, I think both representing the spirit of the protection of minorities in the House and also, I think, the generosity of the House, that what those members are entitled to can be given to them with a generosity and a recognition that respects the fact that they are members of a political party, so long as it does not give them an advantage that they would not otherwise enjoy as five members and, secondly, so long as it does not deprive other members of their right to participate in some way.

Let me extend that thinking so that there can be no doubt about it. For example, if this were a Wednesday and we were concluding debate at six o'clock, it would seem to me that to recognize a member of the Social Credit party at this time would be to give them a right which they would not otherwise enjoy because the debate would stop at six. It would give them a participation in the debate which is disproportionate to the presence of five members in the House.

On the other hand, this debate is not going to stop at six o'clock: it is going to stop at 9:45 p.m. I therefore take this view, as I have done in question period, that members of the Social Credit party are not entitled to put a questioner up every day. They are entitled to two out of three or perhaps three out of five in a week. It seems to me, however, that the sensible and proper thing for the Chair to want to do, giving them only what they are entitled to, is to try to give the opportunity to them in such a way as to recognize the existence of a political party. It is not something that the House can simply wipe out of existence.

Similarly, today when I see on the list that in rotation the hon. member for Beauce is going to address the House in this debate, it is therefore to no cost of other hon. members in terms of participation for the House to take the generous attitude that he ought to be treated as a party leader, which he is.

Some hon. Members: Hear, hear!

Mr. Speaker: Therefore, guarding always the position that I must examine and that no privileges can be given to that party which might unfairly cost the participation of other hon. members, always when I can I ought to try to give them their fair participation and fair share in that way. Again I say that in the question period not every day shall it follow right after the participation of a New Democratic party member, but some days it will. Other days, as it did today, it will come later in the question period. Where possible I think the House ought to extend at least the generosity to give members of that party what they are justly entitled to, but to give it to them wherever possible in such a way as to recognize their position as, in fact, a political party in Canada.

For that reason I therefore now give the floor to the hon. member for Beauce (Mr. Roy).

The Liberals were incensed! They had been trying for years to win this battle of Quebec representation. Having now come within five seats of total triumph over the Social Credit, they did not see this in any way as a mere question of civility. The Liberal House Leader, Mr. Yvon Pinard (Drummond), rose on a point of order to move that Mr. Fabien Roy not be heard, but that instead The Hon. Member for Winnipeg-Fort Garry (Mr. Lloyd Axworthy) be recognized. I declined to hear him for two reasons: first, because he was attempting to introduce a motion when he only had the floor on a point of order, and, second, because in this case, I had done more than simply recognize the Member—I had given specific reasons for doing so. Therefore a motion to the contrary would constitute an appeal from the Speaker's ruling, which is expressly prohibited.

Both rulings were on very thin ground. Standing Order 29 is the rule which specifically provides for such a motion:

When two or more members rise to speak, Mr. Speaker calls upon the member who first rose in his place; but a motion may be made that any member who has risen "be now heard", or "do now speak," which motion shall be forthwith put without debate.

Since by its very terms, it is only to be used to protest the recognition of a Member already announced by the Chair, there is no other way it can be done except by a point of order. A better decision on my part would have been to accept the motion and allow it to be put to a vote. As such, it directly contradicted a very basic procedural precept that a motion can only be introduced during debate by a Member who already has the floor. I draw some consolation from the fact that many Commonwealth Speakers, as I did, have asked that the conflict be considered by the Procedure Committee.

Had the matter been confined to a procedural squabble over

the proper rotation for participants in this debate, it wouldn't have been too bad. Unhappily, it very quickly got much worse.

The following morning, November 7, Mr. Pinard raised a question of privilege based upon an article on the front page of *The Globe and Mail* of that morning which stated in part:

> Mr. Baker said in an interview that he made some representations to Speaker James Jerome because he was moved by Socred Adrien Lambert's look of genuine outrage when the five member Quebec party recently walked out of the House in protest.
> Mr. Jerome granted Mr. Roy "the generosity of the House" yesterday and allowed him to speak immediately after the three party leaders –

A suggestion from the Government House Leader about virtually any aspect of House business would not normally be an extraordinary occurrence, although it would be automatically understood that if I were to consider it seriously, I would advise the House Leaders of other parties, which I did in this case. It would be improper for any one House Leader to make a representation on behalf of any Member or party, unless it were made to me in the presence of the other House Leaders. Any suggestion of a claim to have persuaded me privately to help them would have been a very serious breach of propriety. We were therefore into a very important question of privilege indeed.

The argument took the entire afternoon of November 7, and involved some very sensitive allegations. This is the full text of my disposition of the matter later that day:

> We have been dealing so far with the questions raised by the hon. member for Drummond and the hon. member for Papineau relating to an article which appeared in *The Globe and Mail* yesterday. The question raised by the hon. member for Cape Breton Highlands-Canso does not touch upon *The Globe and Mail* itself. The matter raised is a matter which the House, of course, takes seriously. I also take it very seriously, and I think the House has had a very extensive discussion. Yet, perhaps because this is a minority Parliament, we can

feel ourselves under an obligation to be extremely cautious about things of this sort.

Perhaps over five years as the Speaker dealing with members who now are party leaders in this House—although two of them have changed seats—because we came to know each other there would be a natural tendency toward informality in our discussions. That is only natural, and I think a trust and confidence was built up during that time which it is only natural for me and other members to rely upon and perhaps to take for granted. I am absolutely satisfied that what the President of Privy Council was doing on this occasion was speaking to me in a way he did many times as opposition House leader in the last Parliament.

I do not set aside lightly the points raised. They are very serious, and I know the hon. member takes it seriously when he apologizes to the House. If in any way—even as I think the hon. member for Pontiac-Gatineau-Labelle (Mr. Lefebvre) said in his last intervention; I think he used the word "inadvertently"—in his suggestion on that day he had put me in an awkward position and in turn put the House in an awkward position, he again apologizes for that.

The hon. member for Papineau said that the third intervention by the President of Privy Council (Mr. Baker) was better than the first two. Perhaps, then, we can just concentrate on that one. The President of Privy Council, it seems to me, at least in that intervention—that is the one I remember best because it was the most recent—said first of all that if the quality of the report in *The Globe and Mail* is not what it should be, he accepts responsibility for that and lays the blame on his inadequate expression to the reporter. I am paraphrasing, but he accepts that.

Second, if his making a suggestion to me, which I subsequently discussed on that same day with representatives of all parties, was seen at any time as a representation which was improper in any way, he apologizes for that. If in the future conduct is such that we must be more scrupulous between the parties in that regard, which has been suggested—that is to say, all members and the Chair—it is something which I think all members would regret.

I think it again indicates to us that in a minority situation where the representations are so close and the situation so fragile perhaps we do have to be a little more formal, a little more careful, exercise more caution and perhaps less friendliness and informality. I hope that is not the case, but in any event I accept—as I am sure the House does—the intervention of the President of Privy Council, who says he intended no such influence, would never dream that such would be taken by me in that context, and that he had only the intention of making a suggestion knowing it would be discussed at a meeting later that day which in fact took place and at which all parties were represented. I am sure the House accepts that. Perhaps, however, the one benefit from this discussion is that we are cautioned to be extremely careful about all these matters.

I close finally by returning to the point of the hon. member for Drummond who raised, I thought and as I indicated earlier, a very valid point relating to the use of Standing Order 29. For the benefit of those who are puzzled by the application I made of it yesterday, I can indicate that it is my understanding that when the Chair makes a selection as envisaged by that rule, a member can only seek the floor to question that by putting, on a point of order, the motion which is contained in Standing Order 29.

I have given the hon. member my reasons for not allowing him to do that yesterday. I was attempting to settle a problem which had been outstanding in the House for quite some time, so I was more than just recognizing a member for debate; I was also deciding a procedural point which I thought ought not to be the subject of appeal by the House at that time. These two rules came in conflict, and I had to decide rather quickly how to apply them, and I did; but I think the hon. member might be comforted by knowing that if in future he wishes to take advantage of Standing Order 29, he should do it in exactly the way he tried to do it yesterday.

I might also point out in conclusion—and I thought I should put the substantive matters forward first—that since by neither motion am I asked to take any particular action on procedural grounds—I have no motion before me to consider, in other words—I therefore set aside the questions of privilege on the basis of dispositions I have just made.

I can't help but feel that the Opposition stopped short of a formal motion containing a specific accusation because in the final analysis they accepted Mr. Baker's word that all of this was done in good faith.

The R.C.M.P. Bombshell

The entire third session, which opened on October 18, 1977, was entirely dominated by one single subject—the Royal Canadian Mounted Police. The release of information about alleged R.C.M.P. law-breaking and cover-up fell like a bomb in the House. For one whole year the subject held the floor in a way unmatched in my memory. It occupied the major part of Question Period day after day, all winter long, and certainly produced many more procedural battles than any other subject during my six years as Speaker.

October 31, 1977, was no exception. On that day, one of the Members who had played a prominent role in the questioning about R.C.M.P. wrong-doing, Mr. Elmer MacKay (Central Nova), brought about the most electrifying moment after Question Period, when he intervened to tell a stunned House:

> Because of some of the circumstances, I thought it prudent to retain the services of an electronics expert to check my office, and I have been told that there is a live recording device hidden in one of the chairs in my office, a device that is fully operative. I thought this might be of some interest to the House. . . .

I immediately assured the House that I would have our House security staff carry out a full investigation, and did so. Ironically, we would have normally turned to the R.C.M.P. for assistance in such a matter, but that was hardly considered suitable, so we called in the Ottawa City Police. As the investigation was getting under-way, The Hon. Leader of the Opposition (Mr. Clark) added this on November 3:

> Immediately following the revelations of the hon. member for Central Nova on Monday of this week, officials of my

office authorized an examination of the offices of the Leader of her Majesty's Loyal Opposition. We received this morning a report of the professional firm undertaking that examination. They report the discovery of a device within a telephone in the conference room of the Leader of the Opposition. The firm advises that —

> The conference room telephone was capable of being used as an eavesdropping device and, in fact, still was capable of being an eavesdropping device until 8:10 p.m. on Monday, October 31, 1977.

We were already well into an electronic sweep of almost every Member's offices—all with negative results. During all of this, the air was filled with innuendo and accusations of every sort, including an R.C.M.P. plot, and self-arranged publicity stunts by Members of political parties. They all formed part of what had become a non-stop daily wrangle that set the tone for the entire fall session. It was not uncommon to spend two and three hours after Question Period, on several consecutive days, sorting it all out—before getting on with the business of the day. I made a number of interim reports to the House on the investigation which was still in progress during the Easter recess in 1978, when suddenly the McKay eavesdropping episode came to a surprise ending. The Toronto investigators retained to do the original sweep had apparently concocted the whole thing as a very enterprising hoax to get their name on the front pages. On April 3, 1978, I was happy to close the book on it by reporting to the House that they were facing criminal charges!

Two New Questions of Privilege
The R.C.M.P. era produced two questions of privilege which broke new ground. Before turning to them, there are some misconceptions about privilege which should be cleared up. Above all, privilege has nothing to do with any notion of exalted status. Quite the contrary, it flows solely from the Member's obligations to his electorate and to Parliament, and it has always been given a very restrictive interpretation—virtually confined to physically impeding a Member's ability to get to the Chamber or to cast his vote. Since such interference would equally impede the course of

House business, there is often an element of contempt of Parliament involved, although they are separate concepts. Similar principles are involved in the concept of ministerial responsibility, to which a Member's grievance is very frequently directed. Every Minister is responsible to Parliament for the full range of his Ministry, and in the face of any unacceptable performance by his senior public servants, will be expected either to dismiss them or resign. An allegation that a Minister in discharging that responsibility has conveyed misleading information to the House is, of course, most serious, and is usually raised in the form of a question of privilege.

Again, contrary to widespread belief, the Speaker does not make a final decision in such questions, but only an initial or preliminary determination of whether the matter appears to fall within the normal limits of Parliamentary privilege. If it does, at the House's insistence of course, it will take priority over other business, and, accordingly, the grieving Member will be allowed to present his motion immediately, without the usual notice. If that does occur, the motion is subject to debate and vote so that the final decision rests with the House.

The outpouring of information about illegal R.C.M.P. tactics precipitated at least two questions of privilege on entirely new grounds: their electronic surveillance of a Member of the House of Commons, and their deliberate deception of a Solicitor-General for the purpose of concealing information from the House.

The first of these new questions was raised by Mr. John Rodriguez (Nickel Belt) on March 1, 1978:

> Mr. Speaker, I rise on what I consider to be a very serious matter of privilege. A week ago in this House it was brought to our attention that two of the members of this House had been the objects of electronic surveillance. Subsequent to that disclosure the Solicitor General (Mr. Blais) confirmed in the House that the person responsible for this surveillance had been in the employ of the Royal Canadian Mounted Police. The person responsible for the surveillance also admitted on national television that he had conducted a bugging operation against me at one point in my riding.
>
> This would clearly indicate to me a breach of privilege if for no other reason than the fact that this calls into question

the privacy of communication between a member of parliament and his constituents, and as such clearly inhibits the ability of a member of parliament to perform his duties.

I would also like to refer your attention, Mr. Speaker, to the statement of Mr. Speaker on October 17, 1973, when he said in this House that an incident of electronic surveillance against the caucus of the New Democratic Party was, and I quote: "A prima facie case of breach of privilege."

I might add that even more weight must be given to this question of privilege because since that time we have had the assurance of the Prime Minister (Mr. Trudeau) that no member of parliament had been the subject of electronic surveillance by our federal police force since the case of Fred Rose.

Mr. Speaker, it is your role to protect the rights and privileges of members of parliament, and it is to you I turn for redress on this matter. I must ask you in that role to obtain any tapes or other objects resulting from electronic surveillance against myself from whatever level or organization under the Solicitor General which is presently holding that material. I must also ask you in your role as Mr. Speaker to discover why that electronic surveillance operation was undertaken, why I was never informed that the operation had taken place, and why the tapes have not been turned over to me.

Since it has now been seven days since this information became public and I have received neither an apology nor an explanation, I must now, Mr. Speaker, ask you to step into this affair. Notwithstanding the action which I have asked Your Honour to take in this matter, I reserve my right to move a motion of privilege at some future time.

The next day, the Hon. J.J. Blais, Solicitor-General, made the initial counter-argument:

Mr. Speaker, I rise to speak on the question of privilege raised by the honourable member from Nickel Belt yesterday. I wish to advise you Mr. Speaker, and through you, members of this House that I am informed by the R.C.M.P. that no authorization was ever given to Warren Hart to conduct electronic surveillance of any member of parliament.

The R.C.M.P. advised me that they do not have any tape or any record of tape existing of a conversation between one of Mr. Hart's targets and the member for Nickel Belt. Obviously, Mr. Speaker, it is impossible for me to turn over any tapes or transcripts to you or to the honourable member because if they exist they were never in the possession of the R.C.M.P.

In view of this reply, Mr. Speaker, the other concerns of the honourable member as to the reasons for the undertaking of an electronic surveillance and to why he was not informed do not apply.

On March 9, I made a preliminary ruling in which I dealt with some procedural flaws in the form of the motion. I invited the Member to present a re-drafted motion because I felt that the point was too important to be lost on a technicality:

However, some questions remain that are of fundamental importance to the House, because I think it is possible to visualize events which have taken place which, although entirely consistent with the assurances given by the Solicitor General to the House, and entirely consistent with the investigation which he undertook and with the results of the R.C.M.P. investigation, may still leave questions to which the House may want to address itself.

I think I should stress here that the role of the Chair, if there are questions about the surveillance of a member, is very difficult. Perhaps the surveillance did take place in the orbit which is classically the privilege of a member, but the possibility of some connection with official surveillance of any sort seems to me to be very close to questions with which the House would want to come to grips, and it is not the function of the Chair to prevent the House from attempting to deliberate on matters which come reasonably close to being questions of substance.

On March 16, Mr. Rodriguez presented the following revised motion:

That the allegation by one Warren Hart, in a sworn affidavit that he taped electronically, on one or more occasions, the member for Nickel Belt, together with the admission by the Solicitor General that the said Warren Hart was for a time in the employ of the R.C.M.P., be referred to the Standing Committee on Privileges and Elections for the purpose of inquiring into the said allegation and the circumstances relating to any such electronic surveillance of the said member, including an inquiry as to what happened to any tapes of the said member that may have been made by the said Warren Hart.

My decision was rendered on March 21:

On the face of it, it seems to me that the electronic surveillance of a member could be regarded as a form of harassment, or obstruction, or molestation, or intimidation of a member, all of which phrases have been used in our precedents to support the position that such conduct is a contempt of the House. In this case I confess that the novelty of the basic problem, the ingredient that though it happened outside the precincts of parliament that it did occur while the agent allegedly, according to his sworn statement, was under contract to the national police force, are aspects which leave me in considerable doubt.

We have already established the fact that this was not a conflict between statements made or assurances given by the Solicitor General (Mr. Blais) to the hon. member with respect to the fact that this man was under no instructions to carry out this form of activity. Nevertheless, there is the ingredient that he was under contract. This has been established and it raises a number of elements which, frankly, puzzle me in deciding whether or not in these circumstances electronic surveillance of the sort alleged might be considered by the House to be an infringement of the privileges or a harassment or a molestation of one of its members in keeping with the terminology used in the past when electronic surveillance did not exist.

That is the position in which I find myself here. In all the circumstances, I hesitate very much to take away on procedural grounds the possibility of reaching a decision on a subject to which the House might wish to address itself. In debating the motion put forward by the hon. member, members of the House might make valuable contributions to the question of whether or not we should treat this kind of electronic interference in some special way.

Indeed, if the House decides in its wisdom that the matter should be referred to a committee for consideration, the committee hearing might result in an indication of the proper attitude which should be taken toward the matter. Therefore, on balance, in the special circumstances which exist here, it is my conclusion that I should resolve my doubt in favour of putting the question to the House at the proper time.

Later that day, there was a recorded vote and the motion was defeated.

The other new question of privilege was raised on November 3, 1978, by Mr. Allan Lawrence (Northumberland-Durham). It involved deliberate deception of the Solicitor-General by the R.C.M.P. on the subject of interception of private mail. In summary, the Member had written, some years earlier, to the then Solicitor-General on behalf of a constituent who had raised a direct and very serious concern about R.C.M.P. interference with his mail. The response contained this sentence:

I have been assured by the R.C.M.P. that it is not their practice to intercept the private mail of anyone and I trust that the above explanation will set your constituent's mind at ease.

As a result, Mr. Lawrence argued that his own subsequent handling of the entire problem on behalf of his constituent was severely prejudiced. Then, during the McDonald Royal Commission hearings into alleged R.C.M.P. wrong-doing, specifically on October 24, 1978, evidence was adduced showing that the R.C.M.P. not only did open mail, but in addition that they deliberately denied it when asked for information by the Solicitor-General, the Minister responsible to Parliament for the R.C.M.P. The point, therefore, went beyond an allegation that the Minister had misled the House. On the contrary, it was acknowledged that the

Minister had acted in good faith, but was as much a victim as the grieving Member. The argument was very comprehensive and was spread over several days.

On December 6, 1978, I spent some time summarizing the discussions and dealing with some concerns about the form of the motion which, at my suggestion, had been resolved with some advice from the Table Officers to Mr. Lawrence, who ultimately proceeded with the revised text of his original motion. The balance of my ruling follows:

> The complaint which is the subject matter of the question of privilege is not directly a complaint about the Minister. Indeed, it is founded on the fact that it is one of the Minister's officials who has calculated to contrive this deliberate deception of the House. In fact, I have indicated some concern about the fact that this may perhaps be looked upon as a new departure in our practice—that we are going around the Minister to get directly at the official by way of this question of privilege. Even if that is so, I have come to the conclusion that it is not a procedural basis upon which I can intervene. Once again, it is a matter to which the House can address itself in debate and in amendment, if necessary, or in a vote. These are not the matters that finally become my responsibility from a procedural point of view, however.
>
> Failing any argument to the contrary, therefore, I would consider that I had dealt with the ancillary matters completely that I listed on November 9. That leaves us with the complaint of the honourable Member for Northumberland-Durham that the testimony of former Commissioner Higgitt . . . leads us to the conclusion that by virtue of an act or omission, the House or a Member has directly or indirectly been impeded in the performance of its functions or his duty or that there has been a tendency to produce such result.
>
> If I so find, then I really have no choice but to find *prima facie*, that a contempt has been committed.
>
> Having considered the whole question with extreme care, I come back to the simple testimony of former Commissioner Higgitt when he said:

That is not, that is not an assurance the R.C.M.P. is giving to the minister at all, and as a matter of fact, the practice was in matters of this kind—the practice was very often ministers' letters were not exactly drafted on precise statements of fact.

I can interpret that testimony in no other way than meaning that a deliberate attempt was made to obstruct the Minister in the performance of his duties and, consequently, to obstruct the House itself.

Even beyond the precedents and the complex law of privilege, I cannot conceive that there is any one of us who would accept the argument that this House of Commons has no recourse in the face of such an attempt to obstruct by offering admittedly misleading information.

I, therefore, find a *prima facie* case of contempt against the House of Commons.

May I, once again, reiterate the consequences of that decision. The job that I have in matters of privilege is a preliminary, procedural review of the matter to determine whether in fact it touches the privileges of Members of the House of Commons or of the House itself. Having done so, I concluded that the motion put forward by the honourable Member must therefore be given immediate priority and taken into consideration by the House of Commons.

The House itself makes the decision on whether the motion shall carry, whether it shall be amended, or if in any way altered, and in fact, whether there is a contempt. I do not make that decision; the House does. I simply want to leave these matters with the House in the way that I am doing and indicate that having reviewed all the matters very carefully and considered all the precedents and arguments very thoroughly, I have come to the conclusion that the honourable Member does in fact have a *prima facie* case of privilege involving a deliberate attempt to impede the House in its work, and perhaps the Minister and, in turn, the honourable Member for Northumberland-Durham.

Having done so, and having collaborated with the honourable Member to a certain extent on the form of the motion, the motion which the honourable Member hands to me at this time follows.

> That the letter sent by the Solicitor General of the day to the Hon. Member for Northumberland-Durham on December 4, 1973, and the testimony of former R.C.M.P. Commissioner Higgitt on October 24 and November 1, 1978, before the royal commission of inquiry (McDonald commission) concerning the practice of the R.C.M.P. in preparing letters for the signature of the Solicitor General, be referred to the Standing Committee on Privileges and Elections for investigation and report.

Here again, the motion was debated, but did not carry the vote. In both of these very difficult questions, the debate and the vote underscore the fact that it is the House that makes the final decision and not the Speaker.

Unanimous Consent

No assembly can function without some kind of unanimous consent escape rule. No matter how carefully drafted and intelligent the procedural laws may be, there will always be situations where the entire assembly becomes trapped and paralyzed, unable to achieve an obviously desirable result. The original intent of the rule (Standing Order 43) was to assist the Government in reacting to consensus emerging from debate. It is frequently used when the House wants to make a gesture of support in a crisis, whether international or domestic, and, as an example, was used in the motion to censure *The Globe and Mail*, to which I referred earlier.

As soon as it was written into the rules that with unanimous consent a motion could be introduced without prior notice, it quickly became part of the arsenal of the Opposition back-bencher. As such, with more and more frequent use, it ultimately became a daily agenda item—certainly a far cry from the original concept. Used in this way, the practice was filled with flaws. It survived only because it acted as a safety valve, which underlines again the basic theme of this part of the book: there must be such mechanisms, no matter how imperfect, by which individual Members can triumph over the system, which so often seems to be structured just to keep them frustrated. Eliminate these safety valves entirely and you invite chaos.

When I took the Chair in 1974, the practice was to call this item after Question Period, so there was in theory no limit on the number of attempts to use it each day. In fact, within the first few weeks, first the N.D.P. and later the Social Credit caucus put forth a team effort to use up the entire day on them. I could only listen to each proposed motion, and then, after every Member had taken one turn, to gently but firmly indicate that an attempt at a second round would convince me of bad faith–"three more and that will be all."

I am happy to say that the House, in an inspired move, later re-scheduled these motions into a fixed time period before Question Period, so that it became largely self-policing because of the time factor; but it still remained a very weak procedure. A Member would get the floor "in accordance with Standing Order 43, to ask the unanimous consent of the House so that a motion may be presented on a matter or urgent and pressing necessity" (which likely had been identified in a preamble). I would then ask if there was the required consent and invariably Members would say NO. The whole process was widely misunderstood: what was being sought was not so much a consent to each motion, but simply to introduce it without the normal notice. Almost no one appreciated that if presented, the motion was debatable. Those who withheld consent felt embarrassed because they had no opportunity to say why. Most resented the dilemma that while bills must receive three readings, they were asked daily to take a stand on controversial questions without discussion. Finally, the Government has to constantly fight the calendar and the clock, while the House scrutinizes and decides on its programme and policies. It is thereby compelled to resist even the slightest chance of those precious hours being given over to anything else. Thus the Government Whip or House Leader felt obliged to shout their rejection of these requests every day. In turn, Opposition Members would often do the same any time the Government seeks consent, just to get even.

I always felt that these motions had no place on the regular agenda, and they only survived because there were insufficient proper opportunities for Members to confront the Cabinet directly on urgent problems. I was happy to see that, early in the

32nd Parliament, they were dropped in favour of Statements by Members. These occur in the same pre-question period time-slot, and allow a few M.P.'s to draw the attention of the House to a grievance by way of a 90-second comment.

Emergency Debates

By contrast, the rule dealing with emergency debates (Standing Order 26) is excellent. Any Member who feels the House should engage in a special debate on an emergency situation must first give the Speaker notice in writing more than one hour before the daily sitting. Immediately after Question Period, the Speaker must rule on whether it is a genuine emergency and, if so, whether it is appropriate that the House hold a special debate—bearing in mind other opportunities that may arise in the House's regular schedule. This preliminary ruling virtually eliminates any abuse of the rule. Furthermore, if the Speaker decides in the affirmative, the debate may be ordered to commence on an evening when the House does not sit, so that there is no interference with regular business. Even the form of the motion is useful. It is simply an expanded motion for adjournment of the House so procedural worries about exact wording are kept to a minimum. Of course, there is never any need for a vote—it is the discussion that counts.

This is not to say that political or personal cunning of Members went by the board—far from it, as I hope you will see from what follows. The challenge for Members was to portray local or isolated problems as national emergencies, and thereby to draw the Government into a high profile debate on an embarrassing situation. Repeated requests for debate in the face of continuing turmoil in any part of Canada were not uncommon—nor were applications sponsored by Members of the two Opposition parties, and sometimes the Party Leaders.

Obviously, too generous an interpretation on my part would destroy the usefulness of the rule; too strict an attitude would only increase the ever present feeling of Opposition frustration. I was also specifically directed by the rule not to schedule special debate if the House had ample opportunity for discussion of the topic in the ordinary course of House business. The debates, when allowed, were always very relevant and, obviously, on timely and important subjects. Thus, on balance, I probably had a more relaxed attitude about them than most of my predecessors, although the Opposition parties might not be quick to agree. You can make your own assessments. I have summarized a few of them, which should give a pretty good idea of the kind of enjoyable challenge I had when Members made intelligent use of a basically sound practice.

Among those I granted: on April 16, 1975, the Hon. Member for Bellechasse (Mr. Adrien Lambert) sought an emergency debate on the Longshoremen's strike which had been tying up the ports of Montreal, Trois-Rivières, and Quebec City. Since the situation had not improved since the previous week, when I had turned down the initial motion for debate, I thought it appropriate to grant the request.

Similarly, on November 17, 1975, I granted an application by the Conservative Member for Vancouver Quadra (Mr. William Clarke) because it was the second request after a week's interval concerning a postal strike.

On February 18, 1976, the leader of the N.D.P. (Mr. Broadbent) sought an emergency debate on the decision of the Canadian Labour Congress to withdraw from all areas of cooperation with the federal government as a protest against their inability to appeal judgments of the Anti-Inflation Board. The matter concerned a long-standing labour dispute with Irving Pulp and Paper in respect to which I had turned down four earlier requests for debate on the basis that it was essentially a matter between a private union and a private employer. However, in view of the action by the Canadian Labour Congress and the lack of any opportunity for Members to pronounce themselves on such a serious development and its effect on anti-inflation measures, I thought it was appropriate that the House have the chance to debate the matter on an emergency basis.

On June 20, 1977, I also granted an application by Mr. Broadbent concerning the possibility of a conspiracy to conceal evidence arising from an illegal break-in by police officers at the Agence de Presse Libre, especially since the apparent objective of the illegal act was the seizure of membership lists of a Canadian political party.

In early 1978, there were several such applications for emergency debate as the value of the Canadian dollar steadily declined, and I set them aside as being more in the nature of a continuing economic problem.

On February 22, 1978, however, I felt obliged to accede to a similar request in two separate applications, which I asked to be combined so that one motion was moved by Opposition Leader Clark and seconded by N.D.P. Leader Broadbent. Ordinarily, inflation and, in particular, rising food prices would not be the subject of an emergency debate. But in October of 1974, when a number of Quebec farmers slaughtered their cattle in protest, I considered that to be sufficient grounds to bring the matter within the exceptional conditions contemplated by the rule. In the same way, when the bomb concerning R.C.M.P. wrong-doings dropped in October, 1977, the revelations of Friday, October 8 by Solicitor-General Francis Fox were, of course, followed by immediate applications by both Opposition leaders.

I accepted the application on the basis that while "emergency" usually applied to a sudden or unexpected occurrence, it can also apply to a sudden and unexpected revelation of events of the past in that they might precipitate a course of conduct which, if allowed to continue unchecked, could certainly precipitate a crisis.

Regrettably, the number of requests turned down far exceeded those accepted. On January 28, 1975, I turned down an application by Mr. Benjamin (Regina-Lake Centre) on the basis that a court decision over-ruling the Canadian Transport Commission on the subject of freight rate increases could not be described in any sense as an emergency. It was the same with Mr. Reynolds (Burnaby-Richmond-Delta) on March 21, 1975, when he attempted to launch a new debate on capital punishment. I also turned down an application on October 25, 1979, by Mr. Robert Andras (Thunder Bay-Nipigon), supported by Mr. Robert Rae (Broadview-Greenwood), when they sought to discuss rising interest rates, on the basis that by way of a specific motion then before a standing committee, and in regular discussions on estimates and budget debate, there would be ample opportunity for it to be discussed in the regular business of the House. In the same way, I set aside one application in November of 1976 to discuss rising unemployment, and another on November 23, 1976 related to the report of the Auditor-General since it was automatically referred to the Standing Committee on Public Accounts. For the same reason, I did not accept an application on November 13, 1978, by Mr. Lawrence (Northumberland-Durham) to discuss Petro-Canada's acquisition of 48 per cent of the shares in Pacific Petroleum Ltd. of Calgary; or by The Hon. Member for Regina-Lake Centre (Mr. Benjamin), on January 23, 1979, concerning the threat to western rural communities from recommendations contained in the Prairie Rail Action Committee report; or the application of Mr. Broadbent, on December 10, 1979, to discuss the Government's decision to export additional reserves of natural gas; or that of Mr. Broadbent, on January 27, 1975, concerning lay-offs in the automotive industry. Again, I repeat, these were turned down because they were continuing problems and because there would be every opportunity for them to be discussed in the course of the regular House business.

Without question, the one that sticks in my memory came in early 1978, when the International Nickel Company announced massive lay-offs in operations in my own constituency of Sudbury, Ontario. It was without question a crisis of the greatest proportions for the entire Sudbury community. In a personal effort to try to avert them, I convened an emergency meeting in my own office of representatives of the industry, together with labour, municipal, provincial, and federal government officials and politicians. To no one's surprise, on February 13, 1978, Mr. Rodriguez, N.D.P. Member for Nickel Belt, the rural constituency that surrounds the city of Sudbury, moved for an emergency debate under the provisions of this Standing Order. I had already declined so many applications in respect to similar problems of a strictly local nature in other parts of Canada, no matter how serious, that I had no choice but to turn this down as well. I don't need to tell you that it made for a very long winter for me in Sudbury!

Looking back over all this, if you have concluded that the chapter title "Games Members Play" is a bit unfair, I cannot disagree. No matter which of these many manoeuvres is involved, nine times out of ten it is used for a very serious purpose and really does not come down to gamesmanship alone. Perhaps I can best illustrate the attitude of Members in this regard by recounting one of my first appearances on national television after my first election as Speaker in 1974. I declined all media invitations for several months to permit me to familiarize myself with my new responsibilities before attempting to explain them to the public. Finally, just before the 1975 Easter recess, I accepted an invitation to appear on Patrick Watson's show "Some Honourable Members" on the C.B.C. network. It was a half-hour interview and one of the questions Mr. Watson asked was about the nervousness I must have felt in the first few weeks, knowing that some of the great procedural experts—for example, Stanley Knowles—would be delighted to catch me off-base. I answered him that, knowing Stanley as I had come to know him over my first seven years as a Member, my guess was that he would get more satisfaction out of giving me helpful advice privately in such a situation than he would out of embarrassing me just for the sake of demonstrating his expertise—and I thought the same was probably true of most experienced responsible Members.

Just after the Easter recess, I bumped into Stanley in the corridor. He stopped to tell me that he had been visiting some friends in Winnipeg and, not surprisingly, had made a point of turning on the programme. Naturally, all ears perked up when the Patrick Watson question was put, and Stanley said something to me I will never forget. He said he could not possibly have been more complimented by my reply.

Many Canadians who watch House proceedings for the first time don't usually have any difficulty accepting that appraisal, but then they ask: if it is such serious business, why don't the Members act like it is? Like many facets of Parliament, there is no single, complete answer, but let me leave you with these thoughts.

Many observers look upon Question Period as all that the House of Commons does, and if they are actually in Ottawa, that is what they come to see. But even with allowances for the procedural squabbles that invariably arise right after, it all consumes, on average, about an hour and a half each day. The remaining four and a half hours are devoted to debate of House business when the decorum is exemplary (it also makes duller spectator viewing). During the, say, 170 sitting days in the average year, the whole range of standing committees is at work examining spending estimates, and in clause-by-clause study of government bills, or upon a specific reference. Apart from the occasional storm, almost every minute of it unfolds in a very orderly fashion. That is not to say that there is any shortage of disagreement—only that the battles are conducted in very civilized fashion. Bear in mind also that unacceptable decorum only occurs in some parts of some Question Periods. That does not excuse it when it does happen, but it is important to recognize that by any measurement, it never exceeds about ten per cent of total sitting time.

Parliament exists to hold the Government accountable in day-to-day confrontations with the elected Opposition. Question Period provides a focus to that exercise which cannot be found in other—perhaps more orderly—assemblies. It is a very highly-charged political arena—one in which the quality of the deportment drops as the partisan by-play rises. Members will never be expected to check all of their political guns at the door, and frankly I don't believe they should. Neither should effective heckling and hard-nosed debate be allowed to give way to rudeness that wouldn't be tolerated anywhere else. But the balance is sometimes not easy to find.

Finally, in terms of Opposition strategy generally, I tend very much to the moderate view that all measures should come to a vote after proper opportunity for discussion. There are many Parliamentary experts whom I consider to be ultra-conservative in their thinking, but who nevertheless stoutly defend the view that Her Majesty's Loyal Opposition must do more than just criticize or amend. Where necessary, not just as a right but as a duty, they must resist with every device available. If a Government bill or policy is bad enough, the weapons of delay, obstruction, filibuster, and boycott must all be used in the hope of compelling the Government to dissolve Parliament and to face the ultimate sanction—at the hands of voters. Of course, that same electoral process equally passes judgment upon the Opposition's performance, and that is exactly as it should be.

There are no easy answers to these questions. Indeed, the subject of Members' behaviour, individually or as a party, leaves me with almost as many questions as answers. I can tell you, however, that the elected Member, and through him or her, the political party, is extremely sensitive to your views, both on questions of substance and form. Members are all provided, at public expense, with a very comprehensive constituency office and support staff programme designed to monitor your opinions, and, believe me, the system works very effectively. The worry is not so much that Members won't try to perform up to your expectations—it is that you won't bother to tell them what those expectations are!

5. Some Major Changes

Television

In any reminiscence of these years, there has to be a place of honour reserved for one milestone I thought we would never reach: the introduction of television in the House. It is not, of course, in the same category as efforts to improve our quality of life or our laws–but as a contribution to the quality of our democracy, it deserves equal acclaim. As such, it is beyond any doubt that we did, in 1977, what most other Western nations were unable to manage. It placed us in the forefront of democratic societies and earned us applause around the world–applause that should be shared by every Canadian.

There is a tendency to think we moved very quickly, but this is only partly true. During my time on the special Procedure Committee of 1968, one of our tasks was to review an extensive study undertaken by our counterparts in the previous Parliament, so the introduction of television had been under active consideration for almost 15 years before it became a reality. Oddly enough, it was the politicians who resisted!

Actually, it may be a bit unfair to call it resistance. As with most problems of this magnitude, it was more a case of a lack of any real consensus in favour, and a great many reasons to be wary: if the networks are allowed in, will everyone have their own cameras and crew? If so, will they all bunch up for the first hour, then go in and out as they please? Will Members therefore "grandstand" to get attention at peak times? And how do you deal with the camera focusing on one empty seat–or several? Will it destroy the dignity of the proceedings? Where do you conceal enough cameras with enough operators? What about the heat–the light?

Unfortunately in this case, House reticence was having a very serious side-effect. Our society has long been conditioned to expect to see important events "live and in colour" in our living-rooms. Deliberations in the House have always been included in this category by the television industry. When they couldn't get in, they had to settle for second best: a wild scramble for interviews in the foyer after Question Period. This arrangement dangerously reversed priorities, so that the actual proceedings of the House before a limited audience became secondary to the post-game session before the cameras. I have no hesitation in saying that this practice was innocently yet steadily contributing to a diminution of the importance of the House in the eyes of the Canadian public and, to a certain extent, in the eyes of the Members themselves.

It had another manifestation. Frequently, Ministers would choose to make major policy statements at a popular location before the cameras rather than to the assembled House of Commons. Whenever that happened, Opposition parties would express their outrage by way of a question of privilege. But always the result would be the same. For example, on November 24, 1976, when the Prime Minister was under attack for making a major policy statement outside the House, I concluded my ruling with the following words:

> That matter has been considered rather fully by the previous Speaker on the occasion to which I have just referred. If honourable Members wish to pursue that and examine the precedent to which Mr. Speaker Lamoureux alluded, there is an even more amplified discussion of exactly the same arguments that were put forward here today.
>
> For the reasons that were applicable at that time I have to conclude that while this forms an interesting debate and while it may very well be valid to make a good deal of the comments—and I stress the word "may"—as to the importance of the subject-matter or as to the courtesy and propriety that may be involved, it is clear, upon the understanding of Parliamentary privilege as it relates to this matter, that it does not and never has extended to compelling a Minister or a Prime Minister to making a statement in the House under any circumstances, regardless of the importance of the subject. Accordingly, adhering to that

precedent, which is crystal clear, and to the nature of Parliamentary privilege, which is very narrow in scope, I have to say that this does not constitute a question of such a nature that it should interrupt the proceedings at this time for the question to be put to the House.

The clarity of that precedent, however, does not alter the basic reality that every time such a preference was shown for the cameras over the House proceedings, Parliament was the loser.

Nor did we get much consolation in 1975 when we authorized what seemed to be an ideal experiment in the hope of getting some answers. A special Joint Committee of the Senate and the House of Commons had been established to deal with illegal drug use, and we arranged to televise some of the Ottawa hearings. Crews were allowed to set up temporary equipment in the Railway Committee Room (the central showcase meeting-room, just off the Hall of Honour in the Centre Block, which derived its name from the famous committee sessions which foreran our national railway legislation). The Senate Speaker, The Hon. Renaude Lapointe, and I ducked in for a moment to see how everything was going. It was unmitigated disaster. The room was full of lights, ladders, cables, cameras, and technicians. From where we stood at the main entrance, we couldn't see or hear any committee members or witnesses—and they were sometimes asked to pause in their testimony for lighting or camera changes. As the final touch, the networks devoted perhaps two minutes of evening news time to coverage of the story—not the committee meeting. The news event was that it had been televised! On the basis of that first try, it is miraculous that we ever went ahead. But as it turned out, it must have helped to plant the idea of the "electronic Hansard"—the concept that contributed more to our ultimate success than any other single factor.

The actual resolution in this matter was the subject of prolonged consultation among House Leaders during the last few months of 1976. Finally, an agreement was reached for two days of debate January 24 and 25, 1977. The House Order of Tuesday, January 25, 1977, was:

ORDERED—That this House approves the radio and television broadcasting of its proceedings and of the proceedings

115

of its committees on the basis of principles similar to those that govern the publication of the printed official reports of debates; and

That a special committee consisting of Mr. Speaker and seven other members to be named at a later date, be appointed to supervise the implementation of this resolution, and in particular

(1) to examine the existing cost and technical studies of building, equipment, personnel and other requirements consequent upon the introduction of radio and television broadcasting of the House of Commons and its committees;
(2) to examine the possible effect of broadcasting on the rights and immunities of members of the House and the rights and protections due to the public; and
(3) to consider whether a period of trial broadcasting, or the broadcasting of special proceedings and debates of the House would assist in the development of permanent facilities and procedures; and

That the committee be authorized to issue such reports on the above as will, in its opinion, facilitate the implementation of his resolution.

After 15 years of caution, why the sudden change of attitude in the House? There are the obvious reasons: the pressure was continually building for this kind of coverage and was bound to come some time. I think, however, there were two extraneous factors that had a great influence on the timing of the decision—one from Quebec City and one from Washington. In Quebec City, the National Assembly had already made the decision to televise their proceedings. With the election of a Separatist government, all Members of the House of Commons became sensitive to the fact that Quebec viewers were tuning in to the Separatist side of the story on daily television without hearing the other side from Ottawa. The Washington factor, of course, had to do with Watergate and the Nixon hearings in the Senate Committee. After the initial shock of the scandal had subsided, it became clear to the North American public that the democratic system would prevail over a failed performance by a President. The role of television in making all of this known to the public took on a profound significance. I believe it couldn't help but have influenced the minds of some of the Members of the House of Commons on the subject.

By putting television coverage on the basis of Hansard, the opening paragraph of the House Order dictated that it be under the control of the House (therefore the Speaker), and that it produce a continuous and verbatim report. By this single stroke, it was hoped that virtually every misgiving would be laid to rest. Happily, in actual operation, it was even better than expected. The cameras very quickly became as much a part of the House as the Hansard reporters. Since they were on all the time, and only actually filming the Member who had the floor (or Mr. Speaker), the game of playing to the cameras never materialized.

The second paragraph of the resolution on television coverage contained two extraordinary features. (These were not in the original draft resolution presented for debate and were added later with my approval.) Committees of the House of Commons, whether standing or special, have prescribed functions under the Standing Orders of the House to examine and conduct clause-by-clause studies of legislation, to scrutinize Government spending estimates and, when directed by the House, to investigate and report. The concept of a committee actually implementing a House resolution was unique–chairmanship by the Speaker made it doubly so. Indeed, there was a good deal of sound advice that it was neither necessary nor desirable for me to commit myself to such a time-consuming project, especially since it could prove very awkward should the mood of the committee turn sour. To be honest, I couldn't resist. Like most Members, once the resolution carried, I was anxious to see it implemented, and to help it along. From a selfish point of view (since it would ultimately be part of my responsibility), I preferred to be with it right from the start. If the atmosphere became hostile, I could always step down. Happily, it never did, and we must have held over 100 meetings. It was one more manifestation of the House of Commons at its best, since every important decision on implementation was taken with approval by consensus of the committee. The first meeting was held on February 28, 1977. By the end of the second session of the 30th Parliament, we had published 13 issues of our proceedings and made five reports to the House, the last one on October 17, 1977, the day before the first televised session. Two weeks earlier, if you had walked with me through the Chamber, you would have bet your life that it couldn't have been done!

As we approached the summer recess in 1977, the committee had progressed to the stage of authorizing the structural changes in the House necessary for television coverage. All parties were agreed that the House would rise July 1 and return October 17, and that that time period was considered to be the absolute minimum necessary for the work to be done in the Chamber. In addition to the reconstruction of the area over the south gallery in order to house the equivalent of a major production studio, we had to rewire the sound system, including every Member's desk. Coincidentaly, the House had amended the law during the prior session to increase the membership and, as a result, the Speaker's Chair had to be moved back about three feet and every desk relocated. Typically, the House breezed past the July 1 date and, in its own inimitable fashion, went on not only through July, but into half of August. What the construction and technical experts said could barely be done in 14 weeks had to be attempted in eight. When the House finally did rise in mid-August, I went home to Sudbury for three weeks.

When I returned after the Labour Day holiday and looked at the Chamber, my heart sank. To put it simply I didn't think Westminster could have looked any worse after the bombing of World War II!

But it did happen. The work continued through the night of October 15, and as the workmen completed the finishing touches on the 16th, the staff and pages conducted a mock session by way of a dress rehearsal for the benefit of the cameramen and technicians. When the Members returned on October 17, the Chamber looked the same as when they had left it two months earlier. With the exception of some glare and heat from original lighting equipment, which was later modified, our first television session the following day miraculously went without a hitch, and continued to do so every day after that.

During the committee sessions, we had been expecting to deal with subjects like operational policy, construction, and cost (five million dollars capital and about $700,000 annually), but I don't think any of us had given a thought to the most important subject that the experts brought up at the first meeting: distribution of the video film to the Canadian public. I, for one, blissfully assumed that our responsibility would end by turning on the cameras. How it got before the viewing audience would surely be a media problem. Indeed, that would have been the case had we simply allowed individual network camera crews access to the proceedings. Instead, under specific direction from the House, the entire operation was to be under House management and was to create an audio-visual record of the proceedings, an electronic Hansard if you will. That concept was the major factor in the success of the operation, and had eliminated almost all of the anxieties voiced by Members during the debate. What we hadn't realized was that the concept also raised an entirely new question about arrangements for public access. The committee must have spent more than half our time on it, in the course of which another aspect of present-day Canadian communications developed increasing prominence: cable television.

It happens that Canada is more extensively wired for cable distribution than any other country in the world. As a result, it has been possible from the start to think in terms of dedicating entire channels to "live" coverage of House proceedings, as opposed to taped replays or excerpts. In fact, our first effort at distribution was a pilot project with the two cable companies that covered the City of Ottawa. That very quickly spread to Toronto and Montreal, then to other major cities, but for some time it remained a pretty primitive operation—physically transporting film to distribution centres. We continued to deal with that question after television coverage was under way in the House, and ultimately reviewed the far more sophisticated proposals involving the satellite now in use.

The finishing touch on the whole operation was the very high demand for it all across Canada. In particular, the fact than we have been able to respond in such a way that live coverage of Parliament has long since been available in 80 per cent of Canadian households. Most predictions of viewer interest were guarded, some downright pessimistic, but the actual response exceeded even the most wildly optimistic estimate. During the constitutional debate, audience measurement ran at three-quarters of a million—about half the audience for the late evening national news telecasts—a phenomenally high rating. More significantly, even at the time of writing this book, the weekend wrap-up programs (which obviously are only watched by those interested specifically in catching up on the week's events in Parliament) have consistently maintained almost the identical audience measurement! The biggest single factor in the high audience rate is surely Question Period–which happens to combine fundamental Parliamentary democracy with some fairly entertaining viewing. This dynamic exercise in representative government is made even better, and more instructive, when it unfolds under the watchful eye of the public through television.

As a final note, there were, of course, some surprises and some unexpected consequences. For me, one of the surprises was our inability to televise committee meetings. Before the House debate in January of 1977, I was convinced that we would begin on an experimental basis by covering one or two committees and, having learned from that, move on to cover the House. As soon as we began House coverage, it became obvious that we could never cover the standing committees in a similar way for a number of reasons. To begin with, while there are a number of cable channels available to show daily sessions of the House of Commons as they unfold, it is obvious that the same kind of availability could not exist for 14 or 15 standing and special committees. Furthermore, it would have been a financial and practical impossibility to cover all of them, and I for one would not accept the responsibility of picking and choosing between the various committees if that were the option.

The unexpected difficulty came from what I still consider to be an absolutely essential operational policy: that of keeping the camera on the Member who has the floor–or else the Speaker–and nowhere else. Many Members expected that after a couple of sessions the policy would be relaxed and that the camera would have more editorial freedom. When Members crossed the floor and found out later that the camera had not followed their every move, there was pressure to make some changes. The first time a Member was named and ejected from the Chamber, there were similar comments. Let me further illustrate the difficulty. After the 1979 election, the Social Credit Party, having had their numbers greatly reduced, lost their status as a political party in the House of Commons. In their opinion, this was just one more element of frustration in their capacity to operate as a French-speaking entity in the national capital. One day during Question Period, they stood as a group and very respectfully, but deliberately, left the Chamber. They walked the full length of the House, bowed to the Chair, and left by the exit behind the Speaker's Chair. At that time, a former Minister was in the process of putting a question to the Prime Minister, who rose to answer while the episode unfolded. I do not believe there could ever have been any justification in moving the camera from the two participants who had the floor—no matter how fascinating or singular the other event might have been. So in both cases—the very rigid operational policy and the televising of committees—I expect it to be a very long time before any changes are made.

In the end, we did in 18 months what we were told couldn't be done in under three years, and we were the focal point of world attention every step of the way. On October 18, 1977, our first televised session was carried as the final feature length story on two of the three major United States networks' high profile evening news shows. The third followed awhile later, and in every case the theme was the same: the Canadian Parliament was doing it while the American Congress was still talking about it. Shortly after, at a conference of Commonwealth Speakers at Westminster, and at the request of Sir Billy Snedden, Speaker of the Australian House of Representatives, the subject was added as a special agenda item, with the lead-off presentation from Canada. Five years later, when the same conference was convened in Ottawa, I was invited to make a presentation again. My pride at having been associated with such a successful venture in bringing Parliament closer to the people is scarcely concealed—but I think every Canadian should feel the same way.

In a curious and indirect way, the introduction of television returns us to the beginning of the book. Before the cameras were allowed in, the television journalists always complained that their print colleagues had an unfair advantage. In the view of the print media, this was an exaggeration since "still" cameras were also prohibited (and they would have at least provided a source of quality prints, which could have served as background slides for television newscasts). No sooner was television in place, than the representatives of the print media began complaining that they now deserved at least the equal opportunity to dress up their reports with action shots. It had only added insult to injury when, by way of complete reversal, they were forced to resort to still prints or photographs adapted from television film. I asked the Press Gallery to come up with a workable proposal. In late 1978, we started, on a trial basis, using one photographer behind the curtain on each side of the House during Question Period. They were to be from different news service agencies, under a pool arrangement, and generally were to operate under the principles governing the television cameras. As a result, they were there for their first opening of Parliament on October 9, 1979, when I became the first Canadian Speaker to be re-elected after a change of Government—but only one of them caught the shot that appears with the introduction to this book.

Television was not the only major change during those years: we went through similar, although perhaps less dramatic experiences with the entire administration—including security—and with the House pages.

Administration

Very few people have any idea of the extent of the Speaker's administrative responsibility. Certainly, I had not the slightest awareness of it until I took it on. It was soon brought home to me however during the late summer of 1974, when the newly elected Member for Selkirk (Mr. Whiteway) pitched a tent in the corridor of the Confederation Building (one of the five buildings the House of Commons occupies for Members' offices and support services) to call attention to a grievance he wanted to bring to the attention of the press (not the House, of course, because it was not yet sitting). I received word that the Sergeant-at-Arms, Colonel David Currie, whose responsibilities included building management, would check on it personally, have a chat with Mr. Whiteway, and report to me. As it turned out, that was all that was needed because Mr. Whiteway was totally unaware of any disrespect for Parliament or for the Speaker, and immediately put an end to his protest. It certainly handed me a quick awakening to that hidden, yet very heavy responsibility for the entire range of facilities at the disposal of the House of Commons and individual Members in carrying out their official obligations.

At that time, the House employed nearly 3,000 people (including Members and their staff) and the annual expenditure ran close to a hundred million dollars. The cost of Members' travel to and within their constituencies was just over three million dollars, about the same as the telephone bills. The range of support services is impressive: offices and staff for Members both in Ottawa and in the constituency; Library of Parliament and its research service, both among the finest in the world; the renowned Parliamentary restaurant, and others throughout the five buildings; a constabulary big enough for a small city responsible for every aspect of security; a television studio to rival any major network; a reporting and printing service which produces daily, bilingual verbatim reports of House sessions and of all committee meetings. The list goes on: Hansard reporters and editors, translators, pages, messengers, barbers, hairdressers, chauffeurs, and a maintenance corps that worked virtually around the clock. It even includes a carilloneur, a masseur, and a medical team.

In the delegation of all this, the Clerk was responsible for services related directly to the House itself; the Sergeant-at-Arms for building management, restaurants, the Press Gallery, and security; and the Director of Administration for everything else—and we used to meet about twice a month.

At one of our staff meetings in October of 1974, the idea of getting around to visit every area at Christmas time was raised. I was very glad to do this and to give you some idea of the size of the operation, it took the better part of two weeks. I was extremely well received, to say nothing of the educational value for me in understanding how many people performed so many tasks, big and small, to make the place run smoothly. Before we were half-way through the first set of visits, it was obvious that it was going to become an annual event. I have some great memories of spending a few minutes in so many rooms, offices, and operating plants, each touched up with Christmas decorations. But I don't think any of them surpassed the experience of having a dance and a beer with the ladies on the early shift of the cleaning staff. Their party began about 8 a.m., and they caught me on my way in at about 9 o'clock in the morning!

I should also explain how suggestions for improvement in the level of Members' services were handled. Until 1974, this had been dealt with exclusively by the Commissioners of Internal Economy, a committee of four of the Queen's Privy Council, who were also Members of the House and who, by statute, were required, together with the Speaker, to serve in that capacity. The list, customarily communicated to the House by message from the Governor-General within the first week of each session of Parliament, almost invariably consisted of the Government House Leader, the Minister of Finance, the Minister of Public Works, and the President of Treasury Board. Meetings were presided over by the Speaker, and by statute only this body could authorize increased expenditures for Members. At the beginning, the agenda often included requests from individual Members without any indication of the position of their colleagues, and I asked the party Whips if they would try to find some mechanism for measuring cross-party support. Fortunately for me, the House went one better and agreed to refer all requests to the Standing Committee on Management and Members' Services, so I was the first Speaker to benefit from a comprehensive all-party review of all of these matters before having to ask the Commissioners to decide. In a rather unexpected way, it also set the stage for the complete overhaul of the administration of the House of Commons.

I don't claim any special credit for the idea. Anyone close to the House of Commons over those years was aware that in growing like topsy, the administration had allowed quite a number of people to move into senior positions without the benefit of a management training programme. Our grievance procedures were woefully inadequate and would have been considered laughable by any Human Rights organization in that the ultimate appeal was to a board consisting of the very supervisors having final authority over the grievor's promotion.

I really had no specific information about breaches of any regulations by Members of the House of Commons staff except, of course, those that were the subject of formal investigation and which were reported in all the public media. But Members of the House, particularly the Ottawa and Hull area Members, would refer frequently enough to the possibility that it always stayed in the back of my mind. My concern was not so much in tracking down transgressors for punishment or dismissal, as it was in seeing to it that the administration came up to a professional level in every way, and I knew it couldn't be accomplished on a piecemeal or patchwork basis. These considerations all remained very much of a general nature without any specific focus, and yet subconsciously I knew I couldn't finish my term without either doing something about it or at least communicating my concerns to the Members. The event that triggered it all came along in 1978; but even then, it wasn't until almost a year later, and after several discussions with the Management and Members' Services Committee, that it took shape as the springboard to administrative reform.

During the summer of 1978, the Prime Minister announced that he was committed to some two billion dollars in spending cuts and was directing each of his Ministers to produce the necessary proposals. Parliament, of course, is entirely separate and independent from government and remains the master of its own budget, independent of any direction from the President of the Treasury Board. At the same time, I saw it as my responsibility to ensure that if the Members decided to address the question of whether we could achieve similar economies, the information should be available to them. I therefore asked the team of senior officials responsible for the preparation of the annual spending estimates to do a preliminary set, so we could put them before the Standing Committee on Management and Members' Services and let them consider the matter before our final estimates came before them for approval in mid-winter. After several meetings, the committee indicated two things: (1) they were willing to give it serious thought, but didn't think they could do so intelligently without a comprehensive review of House administration; and (2) they were deeply dissatisfied with the quality of responses during the hearings and therefore very concerned about management skills in the most senior positions.

At that time, the Auditor-General of Canada, The late James MacDonnell, was developing the concept of "value-for-money" auditing, dedicated to evaluating the cost-effectiveness of government departments in a way similar to that done in private industry. Up to the MacDonnell era, this concept had never been thought possible, and it is a tribute to the quality of his performance in office that it is now in increasing use all around the world. I happened to know also that James MacDonnell's background with Price Waterhouse had been very much on the management consultant side of their extensive practice, and so I invited him to lunch in the hope of getting his help. I should also mention that, during my first three years, I had become increasingly aware of strains on our administration in several areas, mostly resulting from the fact that every aspect of the House of Commons had undergone explosive increases since 1965— without any corresponding transformation of our administrative practices. In any committee review of our staff situation, I always took the position that we were expected to be exemplary in every way, whether it was equal opportunity for women, bilingualism, industrial relations, social benefits, human rights, or whatever. Over those years, I had developed a kind of uneasiness that under close scrutiny we might not be able to pass the test. Not surprisingly, for almost 100 years the most important single factor in being hired or promoted may very well have been endorsement by a Member of Parliament.

As a personal choice, there was a great deal about the old way that suited me. It engendered a kind of family attitude where almost everyone at every level seemed to me to have an affection for the House of Commons. Whatever problems were caused by the old style of running things, I think they were far outweighed by that kind of dedication which didn't seem to exist anyplace else. But I also knew those "good old days" were numbered and that at the level of sophistication during my term (and obviously increasing with each passing year), the public had a right to demand a professionalism in our personnel practices and in our financial control mechanisms which simply was not there.

We met in March of 1979, and the only preamble I put to Mr. MacDonnell was that he bear in mind some of the special, indeed absolutely singular, aspects of Parliament and its administrative specialization, not the least of which is that final authority rests with a committee of 264 elected Members (now 282), and in which it is never expected that an official of the House, no matter how senior, can dictate to Members what services they should or should not enjoy in discharging their obligations to the people of Canada. I extended the invitation to him (rather than have matters surface in the normal review process several years down the road) in the hope that he would consider Parliament worthy of his own personal and special attention and that we could work together quietly but thoroughly to bring every aspect of our administration up to the highest possible level. In that first meeting, I was relieved—not surprised, but relieved—that he fully understood and accepted all of this and was anxious to get under way without a minute's delay. On April 4, 1979, I wrote him a formal letter of invitation and authorization. His preliminary study took about three months and indicated the need for massive reform, which he felt could only be accomplished by putting in place an interim official who would have a combined administration and comptroller function. We quickly accepted his offer to have his Deputy Auditor-General for Canada, Mr. Rhéal Chatelain, take on that very difficult task. Mr. Chatelain was a perfect choice. Before going on to his post as Auditor-General of the Province of Quebec, he spent two years working endlessly and, in a marvellous combination of professional skill and personal charm, gained the confidence and cooperation of even the most senior people in the House in launching what has now become a totally new administrative structure.

None of this could have been completed as quickly or as effectively had it not been for the personal commitment of my immediate successor, Mme Jeanne Sauvé. She turned to this project with tremendous energy. She spent long hours after the daily sessions in the House, with meticulous attention to detail and a firmness that I could never have accomplished, working on the completion of the temporary phase and hence on to the establishment of the present structures. I should add that she was aided in this by the Clerk, Dr. Beverley Koester, who took a similar approach, and who, among other things, instituted an organizational structure which has permitted all of those in the legislative services to aspire to earn their way to the pinnacle, as Clerk Assistant at the Table of the House, and perhaps in turn, as Clerk of the House of Commons.

Security

At the same time, but for different reasons, we were being pushed into changes in security. This might best be illustrated by going back to an event that happened in 1976. As part of their annual carnival, students at Ottawa University had developed a contest in which the object was to outdo the previous year in some spectacular prank. On February 6, 1976 the students managed to conceal someone in the Peace Tower overnight. When the city awoke next morning, the Peace Tower was adorned with the Stars and Stripes waving proudly in the breeze. This is a portion of a letter I wrote to them:

I understand that it was a student prank as part of the annual University of Ottawa Carnival and certainly was not intended as any lack of respect toward Parliament. You will understand, I am sure, that our concern relates to the security of the buildings and we have to assure that the Members and Senators are able to carry out their duties in an atmosphere free from concern about personal safety. We must also remember that the right of the public to visit their Parliament Buildings without feeling unduly restricted by security measures. We could easily put in place stronger protective measures, but always at the expense of the kind of welcome that every Canadian deserves here. Every time someone takes advantage of our good faith and exposes our security to ridicule, it compels us to review our policies perhaps with a stronger emphasis on security measures or invites us to proceed with criminal charges so that public attention will be directed to the delicate balance we must maintain.

In the case of the Peace Tower flag incident, we quickly chose to continue as in the past, but a similar incident since then has once again raised our concern that if we continue not to react, we might invite a flood of similar problems. The number of times in the future that we can pass over such incidents becomes more and more limited.

We all accept the importance of high spirit in Carnival week but we would like to feel equally that you share our disquiet and in your position of authority on the Student Council, you might take the trouble to impress it upon organizers of the Winter Carnival in future years.

Access to parts of the buildings other than the visitors' areas is now restricted to persons with proper security identification cards, including a photograph. In the light of similar experiences at airports, this is no longer an exceptional measure—but neither is it as comfortable as I always like to think access should be to the Parliament of Canada. This initiation of the change-over from the old to the new was not something that gave me great pleasure. It was simply a responsibility that was long overdue.

While on the subject of major changes, let me mention a minor—but important one. When the family moved to Ottawa after my first year, the first August day we walked into the Centre Block, Barry took one look at the Constables and asked me why they didn't have summer uniforms. The next summer, at her insistence, they were turned out in short sleeve shirts, and they looked fine. It may not have been historic, but I can't tell you how much it did for our relationship with everybody in the buildings for the rest of the time.

House Pages

The final change was the one closest to my heart—the page programme. I was always aware that most provincial legislatures provided the opportunity for students to serve as pages, and I wished we could do the same. I was also concerned that in hiring youngsters from the National Capital region, we tended to make it more comfortable for some school drop-outs, and seemed not to be taking on any young women. Yet, any school-related programme appeared out of the question—unless it was also strictly local—because of the different school systems in each province, and especially because there are no public high schools which provide both schooling and residence. One evening, while we were waiting for a late vote, Alistair Fraser and I were talking about it, as we so often did, and suddenly a light came on: university! Just as they do in the United States. As soon as possible, Alistair got down to Washington. After two days of working with their people, he came back full of enthusiasm. I asked our Members' Services Committee, our Commissioners of Internal Economy, and our senior officials to move immediately in the hope of starting this programme after the 1978 summer recess. It is a measure of their cooperation that it happened so quickly and without a hitch. Mr. Raymond Stokes was seconded from the personnel office and took full responsibility for the initial recruitment and set about immediately to travel across the country, securing the cooperation of federal Members and representatives of provincial legislatures where likely candidates might be discovered.

I was delighted to commence proceedings on March 22, 1978, with the following announcement:

Mr. Speaker: The reason I preempt the time of the House to do this now is because it will relate to some interest members will have relative to possible enrollment dates at universities. I thought I should take a moment to explain this to members, because during the recess information will be going out about it. I thought hon. members ought to be the first to know.

Since coming here it has been an interest of mine, and many others have shared it and many others had it long before that time, that we find a way to encourage young Canadians to participate in the House of Commons by serving as pages here. That was attempted at the high school level and faced great difficulty because of discrepancies and differences in various academic programs throughout the provinces.

A couple of years ago I asked the Clerk of the House of Commons to attend in Washington to examine the system there. He did, and returned with a very thorough report which was referred to the Members' Services Committee. The members of that committee worked very diligently on the project, with great interest, and came up with what I think is an excellent idea. I hope all members will share it. It is that the program, instead of being operative at the high school level, be operative at the first year university level, which facilitates provincial interchange much more easily and enables residents away from home to lead a much more normal course of life.

Having given approval to that basic idea, we are attempting now in some hurry to implement, at least partially, this program before September, which will involve possible enrollment by students in two Ottawa universities, whose co-operation we have received throughout and for which we are very grateful.

I want to assure hon. members on a couple of counts. First, this program will be phased in in such a way as to ensure that all of those who have served so faithfully and well as pages will not in any way be prejudiced or jeopardized in the employment they have enjoyed here.

Some hon. Members: Hear, hear!

Mr. Speaker: The obvious advantages bear some repetition. We will now be able to secure, in addition to this cross-Canada participation, young people for a year of university, for which they will work as pages and receive a full salary which will enable them to finance their education.

We will, of course, benefit from that kind of participation. We will benefit from being able to do something that is long overdue here, that is, to employ an appropriate number of female pages in the House of Commons.

Some hon. Members: Hear, hear!

Mr. Speaker: May I at the same time indicate that we will be giving, in the process, some serious consideration, and I hope that hon. members do not rebel at this, to altering the uniform being worn by pages in the House. While we feel we must maintain the dignity required in the Chamber, it will reflect something that is a little more in keeping with modern times. We have in mind something in the nature of a blazer in the House of Commons green colour, with an appropriate crest, and grey flannels for the boys and skirts for the girls. However, we will receive suggestions from members on that.

The basis of the programme is that students entering university in their home province can instead attend Carleton University or the University of Ottawa in either Arts or Science, without prejudice to their right to advance into second year at home. Both universities provide residence facilities and one is bilingual. The House takes on a sufficient number of students to leave them time to attend class and study, and pays them enough to ensure that they do not lose ground financially. The quota is evenly distributed on the basis of population so as to guarantee representation from every corner of Canada. Needless to say, the concept enabled us in 1978, for the very first time, to see proportionate numbers of young women and men serving as pages in the House.

It is a programme from which everyone benefits. Members of the House of Commons are better served, and they feel in return an obligation to encourage the pages to learn as much as possible from that experience. I don't think it is an exaggeration to say that this investment in these young people becomes an investment in Canada. The photograph with the pages of that first "Class of '78" is one of my most treasured souvenirs—and so much more so since 1983, when I was invited to speak at their 5th Anniversary

Dinner. I spent a marvellous evening in the company of a great number of young Canadians and realized for the first time that there had been one other unexpected, but very substantial additional dividend: together they have found friendships they will cherish all their lives. In the process, they have learned about each other and about our country in a way that couldn't be done in any classroom. They also stay together as a sort of "alumni association" and meet every year under the guidance and encouragement of their "den-mother," Mademoiselle Annette Léger, who has shared the administrative responsibility for the programme since its inception. I hope to share their five-year reunions many, many times.

6. The Permanent Speaker

I remember a conversation with Speaker Lamoureux during the summer of 1974, after my nomination was widely rumoured in Ottawa. The first thing he said to me was that if I became Speaker, I would begin explaining the role the day I was elected and I would never stop. No truer words were ever spoken! Like so many unwritten Parliamentary or constitutional conventions, there is every theoretical reason why our concept of the Speakership cannot work. How can a Speaker serve his constituents when he can't speak on their behalf? How can a Speaker reconcile needed constituency assistance, which of course must come from Cabinet, with the essential principle of objectivity and impartiality and the solemn responsibility to preserve the Opposition's rights to attack the Government? How can a Speaker seek a party nomination and go through an election campaign without criticizing any of the parties in Parliament? How can there be any genuine impartiality when every Speaker since Confederation (until 1979) was the nominee of the party in power? The fact is, again like so many unwritten conventions, that it shouldn't work—but it does.

It is no surprise, however, that there has never been a time, since the very first Parliament, when some suggestion of a formula for a candidate independent of all partisan or political considerations has not been actively pursued. In my earlier reference to the events of September 30, 1974, and my election to the Speakership, I included portions of the speeches of the Party Leaders. Robert Stanfield also dealt very extensively in his remarks of that day with his personal commitment to the concept of a permanent Speaker. He referred to the Lamoureux decision to seek election as an independent candidate in the 1968 election, and said the following:

> For this reason, I asked my party's association in the constituency of Stormont-Dundas not to present any candidate against Mr. Lamoureux at the 1968 election. Following his election, I was honoured and pleased to second his appointment.
>
> The agreement concluded with the Stormont-Dundas association was designed to find other means to succeed in appointing a permanent Speaker and it provided the association with the right to choose a candidate in a new election.
>
> Between the election of 1968 and the election of 1972, the Prime Minister and I had discussions to explore an alternative method of achieving what I had in mind, and what others had in mind, which was a method alternative to that by which the associations in the Speaker's constituency would be denied the right to nominate a candidate. These discussions were not fruitful, much to my regret. Mr. Lamoureux ran in the election of 1972. He was opposed by a candidate from my party. Mr. Lamoureux ran as an independent and was elected. Following the election of 1972, the Prime Minister discussed with me a choice of Speaker and indeed a Deputy Speaker. There was no difficulty and we reached an understanding and agreement. I felt this was a substantial step forward, and compensated in part at least for the earlier failure to agree on a method of securing a permanent Speakership and a method of completely removing the Speaker from partisan politics on his election.

Mr. Stanfield was by no means alone in his thinking. For many years the Order Paper carried a private Member's bill in the name of Stanley Knowles (Winnipeg North Centre), which would permit the House, having first chosen a Speaker from among elected Members, to later have that person represent an artificial constituency—Parliament Hill—thereby allowing the Speaker to continue in office and releasing the constituency for a full-fledged contest. Mr. Knowles was the first Canadian Member of Parliament to be made an honorary lifetime officer of the House of

Commons of Canada. It may not be as well remembered that he very nearly became Speaker.

In the election of 1962, the huge 1958 Diefenbaker majority was reduced to a minority. Regrettably, both for our small fraternity of Speakers and for Canada, one of the casualties was The Right Hon. Roland Michener (Toronto, St. Paul's), who had been a most excellent Speaker in every sense of the word during those four years. His decisions were thorough and comprehensive, and his precedents guided me through difficult situations just as surely and almost as frequently as did the many I took from the Lamoureux era. Very early in his term, he established his independence in rulings against the Government, which incurred the personal displeasure of Mr. Diefenbaker to such an extent that no appointment was made for him during the course of the last Diefenbaker Government in 1962-63. It was only after the change of Government in 1963 that Prime Minister Pearson appointed him first, High Commissioner to India, and ultimately, Governor-General. Had Roland Michener had the good fortune, as both Lucien Lamoureux and I did, to represent a single city constituency, I am sure he would have stayed on as Speaker. But when election swings occur, the tidal wave tends to hit the Metro Toronto ridings first and hardest—so the voters ended any chance of a long and distinguished career for one Speaker, but almost created another.

Faced with a fight for survival, and with no Conservative to spare as his nominee, Mr. Diefenbaker offered the Speakership to Stanley Knowles (Winnipeg North Centre)—a proposal, needless to say, that met with widespread approval. The details of this are for the Knowles story, not mine; but in what must have been one of the greatest agonies of his life, Stanley had to balance his devotion to Parliament and his profound respect for its highest office, against his relentless fight for "his people": the senior citizens, the veterans, the disadvantaged. After much soul-searching, he turned the Speakership down—to Mr. Diefenbaker's astonishment; no, astonishment is not a strong enough word: it was pure outrage, to the point, as I understand it, that Mr. Diefenbaker did not find the occasion to speak to Stanley for almost ten years!

I refer to this story here for two reasons: first, obviously, because it concerns a great parliamentarian who almost joined our small group of Speakers, but also because he was one who was always committed to the concept of a permanent Speaker. It was widely believed at the time that had any commitment been made by Parliament to at least consider that concept, his decision might have been different.

Mr. Speaker René Beaudoin, prior to his tragic self-destruction during the Pipeline Debate's "Black Friday," also had been suggested frequently as the ideal candidate for Canada's first permanent Speaker. In fact, all of us who succeeded him would have been comforted had his demise seemed inevitable, but the truth was exactly the opposite. René Beaudoin was a scholarship student who obtained a degree in law at the University of Montreal. He had worked at almost every conceivable part-time job to finance his education, an experience which intensified his natural empathy with the common people—a great asset for any Member of the House of Commons, especially for the presiding officer. He had served very capably as Deputy Speaker, chaired a committee on procedure, and even started work on a book on the subject. His was the first nomination to be seconded by the Leader of the Opposition (The Hon. George Drew), and in the Chair his reputation for fairness and competence had been growing steadily.

In the famous Pipeline Debate, he tragically lost sight of a most fundamental principle: that the Government is not only distinct from, but, more importantly, is accountable to Parliament. The St. Laurent Government had committed itself to a financing deadline for the pipeline of June 7, 1957, and, as governments frequently do, set out, after the fact, to gain approval of Parliament. In such self-created emergencies, the rules are always under great stress. While it is important that the presiding officer try to accommodate the will of the House so that the rules are there as servants and not masters, it must never be forgotten that the problems, deadlines, or commitments of the Government are not those of the House—and certainly never those of the Speaker. No matter how praiseworthy or essential the objective, decisions of the House must be brought about in conformity with accepted House practices. The consequences of the inability to do so must rest with the Government. It is evident from some of his early comments that Speaker Beaudoin began to look upon June 7 as a deadline for Parliament. On that Black Friday, it is clear that he did so at the expense of his objectivity. Only the Government majority rescued him from a motion of censure for having proposed, of his own initiative from the Chair, that the calendar be turned back 24 hours so as to restore the situation as it had been before he made what he later came to consider as a faulty ruling! A month later, the publication of his personal correspondence critical of the Opposition left him no choice but to resign—a constant reminder for all of us that disaster is never far away, even for one who had been considered the ideal candidate for permanent Speaker.

These concepts were obviously very much in the mind of Lucien Lamoureux when he sought re-election in 1968 and 1972 as an independent candidate. In 1968, the Conservatives agreed not to nominate a candidate, and the Liberals agreed not to nominate either, and also not to actively campaign for Lucien as they had in the previous election. The Government stance was more comfortable, of course, since they expected to be re-elected, and to re-elect the same Speaker, which is precisely what happened. It is far more difficult for the other side. For the local party organization, the election battle is its *raison d'être*, and foregoing that entire contest quickly saps the party lifeblood away— especially when it is in the name of some obscure tradition which Parliament seems unprepared to recognize in any tangible way. It must have been extremely difficult for The Hon. Robert Stanfield to accomplish it in 1968, and obviously impossible to repeat it four years later, when not even a discussion of the concept had occurred in the House in the interim.

For the N.D.P. there have always been two additional problems. As the third ranked party in terms of number, and fighting for growth, the N.D.P. Leader is under heavy pressure to field a candidate in every seat in order to maintain the image of a truly national political force. It is hard to reconcile that militant theme with an agreement not to contest a particular seat. Secondly, the N.D.P. has generally taken the position that the Knowles bill provides the answer. Since the other parties won't even discuss it, why should they pay the price in the Speaker's constituency? As a result, both the Conservatives and the N.D.P. fielded candidates against Mr. Lamoureux in 1972. He ran—again identifying himself on the ballot as an independent, although he had once more the support of the local Liberal organization—and won again, which most people in Stormont-Dundas felt he could have done forever. He essentially took the personal responsibility and a great risk for establishing a Canadian precedent to match the British. But after two tries (1968 and 1972), it seemed Canada simply was not ready.

I, of course, had only a vague awareness of any of this in the two months between my mid-summer meeting with the Prime Minister and the opening of Parliament on September 30, 1974. When the usual post-election Liberal caucus convened for two days in August, I not only came to Ottawa for it, I walked over to the West Block caucus room right to the door—but I didn't go in. As it turned out, I never did again. I knew the Speaker had to divorce himself from any partisan activity, but I was also very sensitive to the fact that I was not yet in the Chair—and couldn't be until the House voted on it. Participating in caucus felt wrong to me, so I didn't—and yet staying away seemed to me to presume that my election was a foregone conclusion.

And as every one of us has done, I began then, and continued for six years, to try to explain—especially to my own voters—the rather delicate relationship between Speaker, political party, Government, and constituency. This interesting phenomenon can't be addressed without some insight into the texture of Canadian constituencies. At the two extremes are the rural and the down-town Metro seats. Some of Canada's rural electoral districts are bigger than most European countries, so that the task for the Member of being "at home" is almost impossible. An event in a town in the south-west corner of the riding which warrants the Member's presence would never come to the attention of the other 75 per cent of the riding. Thus the Member must not only go there every weekend, but in all likelihood will travel more miles inside it than in simply getting there from Ottawa. But there is an enormous compensating factor: rural people identify with their elected representatives and tend to stay with anyone who works hard at looking after them.

By contrast, in the time it takes to drive from the Parliament Buildings to the Ottawa airport, you can walk all around any of the 60 seats that lie in downtown Toronto and Montreal, but it is very unlikely that a Member can do anything to assist any one seat as distinct from the Metropolitan area. As well, there is no semblance of a personal relationship with the voters, half of whom will have moved before the next election.

In between lies the best of both worlds: the single city riding, like mine in Sudbury (it was almost the same with Mr. Lamoureux where his riding was in part rural, but with a dominant city – in his case, Cornwall). There is the same identity factor as in the rural riding, combined with the ease of access of the urban, but above all, there is facility for constant and complete communication. When I was home in Sudbury, I was at home to the whole constituency, and events were covered by media that could reach all of it. When I had something to report from Ottawa, contact with one newspaper and three radio-T.V. services, two English and one French, did it all. Any projects which might help bring jobs or improved services could be understood and seen by everybody in town.

Upon reflection, I am fascinated to find that the similarity between Mr. Lamoureux and me in the physical make-up of our constituencies projected itself into almost identical experiences as we both attempted to bring home some very much needed aid in almost identical economic crises. Cornwall was almost totally dependent for industrial activity upon the textile industry. During the Lamoureux term, pressure from cheap foreign imports just about shut it all down, so that the community's unemployment rate was almost triple the national average. Appropriately then, Cornwall was one of two Ontario communities chosen to launch the first Federal Regional Development Programme.

When I moved to Sudbury in 1958, the population was about 100,000, and 40,000 people were directly engaged in production of what then constituted 75 per cent of the world supply of nickel. In February, 1980, when I stepped down, both nickel producers, INCO and Falconbridge, had been non-operational due to either shut-down or strike for roughly one day out of two in the previous two years, and the total number directly employed in nickel production was only slightly over 10,000. It was against this background in 1976, when the Government announced the programme to decentralize government operations so as to spread the benefits around the country – and, coincidentally, to create some eight or nine regional Taxation Data Centres for the Department of National Revenue – that I made known my expectation that Sudbury must surely form a prime target. Just as Mr. Lamoureux had done in Stormont-Dundas, my success in bringing one of the Taxation Data Centres to Sudbury seems to me to have been due in about equal measure to the near disastrous economic factors, as it was to our added personal power as Speaker—no more, but no less than equal parts. Nevertheless, assistance for the Speaker's constituency, which can only come from the Government, remains a significant factor in any debate on the permanent Speakership.

Because of the Lamoureux example, I assumed from the beginning that I would be expected to run as an independent next time around. Happily there was no hurry, and I had all I could do in the first two years just to cope with my current duties. The first time I even had the chance to introduce the suggestion was on a half-hour interview on television in Sudbury, just prior to the resumption of what many expected would be the last year of the Parliament after the summer recess in 1977. The reaction certainly didn't do anything to simplify matters. Almost no one understood what it was all about, and those who did understand didn't believe it would happen. Very few expected the Conservatives to agree, but then they had always run third behind the N.D.P.—and absolutely no one believed the N.D.P. would hold off. At that time, the Sudbury labour movement still laid claim to one of the biggest locals of the United Steelworkers Union in all of North America, and failure to win my seat for the N.D.P. was not something that brought them great cheer. Nickel Belt, next door, had gone back and forth a number of times between the Liberals and the N.D.P., and I began my own career with a 1967 by-election loss to the N.D.P. by 156 votes, so I would have been surprised if they had shown any interest.

Through to Christmas, I must have been involved in a dozen open-line interviews or public meeting discussions of it, and there was certainly no sign of any enthusiasm for the idea whatsoever. But the real surprise came when I called a meeting of the Sudbury Liberals to give the idea a full airing. To say that the notion was rejected does not do it justice. The truth is that everyone questioned and fought it for every conceivable reason. Obviously, if all parties went along and it amounted to a virtual acclamation, that would be fine. But could I first be sure they would? No, I couldn't. Could they be sure another Liberal wouldn't seek the nomination? No. If there was to be no Liberal candidate on the ballot, would it signify that I was in party disfavour? No, in fact, it was expected that the party leadership—hopefully the Prime Minister personally—would come to Sudbury to ask that the Sudbury Liberal Association decline to nominate, and go out and support me as they had in 1967, 1968, 1972, and 1974. Well, if he can do that, what's wrong with you running as a Liberal? And what about the four or five hundred volunteers from earlier campaigns: do you ask them to try to whip up some kind of campaign spirit with no Liberal signs, posters, literature, no national ads, no nomination convention, and no all-candidates meetings? Are you sure you're not doing it this way because of the sudden drop in popularity for both Trudeau and the Liberal Party? What does it all prove anyway? And finally, Jim, it's taken over three years, but the people of Sudbury are finally getting used to the idea of being represented by the Speaker, and on balance they're accepting your suggestion that we are better served. If you can keep proving it, you'll be okay, but don't ask them to accept this independent candidate theory—they just won't buy it.

This brings us to the Christmas recess of 1977. When the House resumed in January, 1978, which we all thought would be election year, I set out to talk the independent designation over with the Party Leaders. Two took a predictable position, and very much confirmed what I had anticipated. The Prime Minister was kind enough to say that he would always be proud to see me run under a Liberal designation (that was not the predictable part) but that, if I chose instead to follow in Lucien's footsteps, he would do all he had done in both '68 and '72, including the request that the Sudbury Liberals actively campaign on my behalf. The whole thing of course was predicated upon both other parties doing the same thing, which at that point was still an unknown quantity— but not for long.

Very soon after, N.D.P. Leader Ed Broadbent and I had a very thorough and congenial discussion which put the question to rest. It was interesting but idle to talk about his own opinion or mine, or the effect of the Lamoureux experience. Neither of us believed that the Sudbury N.D.P. Association would be the slightest bit interested in staying out of the fight. He did not rule out the possibility if there was first complete agreement with everyone except them. But short of that—and maybe even with it—it would probably embarrass both him and his Sudbury Association to so much as suggest it. He repeated, and I think quite sincerely, that if something along the line of the Knowles concept of a continuing Speaker could be achieved, he would openly endorse my nomination. Short of that, he thought any suggestion that his party—more particularly the Sudbury N.D.P. Association—would forgo the contest in support of some half-way measure was a pious hope.

The conversation with Mr. Stanfield had some surprises. I invited him to lunch in the Speaker's chambers. As soon as he arrived, it was evident that he wanted to clear away any misapprehension that I might have had over his action in not seconding my nomination for Speaker. Bear in mind that this was fully three and a half years later—and take my word on this: when he said on September 30, 1974 that he was acting upon principle and not in any way out of criticism of the choice, with which he did not disagree, I believed him then and still do—and I had never thought of it again. But it is an indication of his own sensitivity that he still wanted to get it off his chest. It is also a sad commentary on political life that we had seen each other many times every week, and within the context of Parliament had come to know each other fairly well, and yet had not had the chance for anything resembling a private conversation in all that time.

I was also pleased and greatly relieved to hear his opinion on how I would run. As already noted, he had given a good deal of thought to his own part in the Lamoureux candidacy. He was far from satisfied that either the public or the Members of the House made a direct connection between independence in the Chair and independence from a party label in an election campaign. Elected Members were perfectly capable of judging the Speaker's impartiality and did so every day. If they didn't believe in it, no Speaker could survive, but specifically, he didn't think my designation on the general election ballot would contribute one way or another to the Members' confidence in my objectivity in the Chair. He reaffirmed his interest in the idea of a permanent Speaker and his willingness to participate in any all-party discussions on it (or on the Lamoureux experience), but basically it was his view, considering such enormous complications for so many people, that it simply wasn't worth it. I can't recall if I was more impressed with the soundness of his reasoning or if I was simply relieved to be released from the horrendous task of selling my people on the principle of the Speaker as an independent candidate.

It was obvious, as so often happens, that we were facing a practical solution to a theoretical problem. None of the Party Leaders was enthusiastic about the independent candidacy, which probably was indicative of a lack of consensus in their party caucus. Without one of them as a driving force, all-party agreement would never occur. I was personally ambivalent—uncomfortable with the idea—yet I had always felt an obligation to continue what Lamoureux had begun, which was why I had raised it—loud and clear, and as often as I could—during the last half of 1977. When reaction in Sudbury and in Parliament ranged from indifferent to violently negative, I finally decided that Mr. Stanfield was right.

I then had to spend another six months getting the Sudbury voters to forget about it, but at least the proposition proved itself in the only test that really matters. In the 1979 election, I ran under the same Liberal Party designation as I had carried in all previous elections. With some allowances for population shifts, my margin of victory was very close to the 10,000 figure which had remained constant through all the elections I contested.

In this context of continuity in office, the summer of 1979 immediately took on great significance. I had no illusions about certain basic realities. A change of Government is not the regular occurrence in Canada that it is in other countries. And all of the elements of our 1979 situation have never come together before in quite the same way in Canada so as to enable a Speaker to serve under two governing parties. Even at that, there would have been enormous pressure upon Prime Minister Clark to symbolize the end of the long period of Conservative drought by putting one of the senior Members of the Conservative caucus in the Chair. Certainly, had it been a majority Government, that pressure would have been irresistible. Even had I been the best Speaker of all time, the historic step might never have been taken. Just as clearly, I knew that many of my former colleagues in the Liberal caucus would resent any decision on my part not to rejoin them. All the more so since in this case, it would help bolster the position of Prime Minister Clark in forming the Government by eliminating the need to reduce his Conservative ranks to nominate a Speaker.

As in 1974, the initial approach came from the Government House Leader, The Hon. Walter Baker. Very soon after the election, he advised me that Prime Minister Clark's personal inclination was to offer me the nomination. Of course, no official position could be taken without a discussion in caucus, which would leave the final decision until quite close to the recall of Parliament. Needless to say, there was ample public and media discussion, but in my own mind there was never much question. Continuing on as Speaker was something I felt I ought to do and very much wanted to do anyway. Out of courtesy, I took the first available opportunity to inform Mr. Trudeau of my decision to continue as Speaker if asked. If there was any dissatisfaction or Liberal caucus consensus to the contrary, he certainly gave me no indication, nor would I have expected him to. In the final analysis, it would be a personal decision on my part. Regardless of party affiliations, I felt everyone on all sides of the House would readily acknowledge that it would be a positive step for the Speakership and therefore for Parliament. Throughout all of it, interestingly enough, and during all of the following Parliament, as short as it was, my Liberal party nomination or designation on the general election ballot was never discussed—it was simply not a factor.

None of this is to say that independence could ever be considered a secondary factor for any Speaker, either in fact or appearance. From that first uncertain experience about going in to the caucus room in August 1974, and forever after, the only time I was in the presence of Members of only one political party was for the discussions I've described elsewhere in this book. No matter how informal the event, I always made sure that if one Member of Parliament was to be there, we invited another from each political party. I never attended so much as a testimonial dinner for any of my former Liberal colleagues, and indeed was never at any party function of any sort. Even in the 1979 election, my campaign literature dealt exclusively with local problems, and in public meetings, on radio or television, I did the same. During the campaign, I never made any reference to the performance of the Government or the Opposition parties. Of course, all of it was confining, but being Speaker also has its own compensating factors, both for the incumbent and for the constituency. No

Speaker can survive without meticulous attention to this principle: there must not only be absolute impartiality in dealings with all parties, there must never be even the slightest appearance to the contrary.

Those who support the status quo of the Speakership in Canada, (and there are a great many experienced Parliamentarians who do) have two very compelling arguments in their favour: one practical, the other mathematical. Any step in the direction of greater independence is aimed, of course, at severing the connection between the Speaker and the Government. It is directed to the fact that in all Canadian Parliaments but one (1979), the Speaker has initially been nominated from within Government ranks. It is also directed to the concern that while in office, the Speaker, like any other Member, can only bring about the best level of service to his constituents with the aid of that same Government. The appearance of dependence upon Government support will always be there, but in actual fact, going back over the last 25 years, it does not seem to have created a problem. Only Speaker Lamoureux and myself needed exceptional assistance for our constituencies, and in both cases, the economic conditions in our ridings were so severe that some special Government help would have been forthcoming in any event. But let us allow that as Speakers we were able to bring about constituency assistance slightly better than average. I never once heard it suggested during my first years in the House that there was any connection between riding assistance and Speaker Lamoureux's attitude toward the government of the day, and I can only assume a similar perception in my own case, although for obvious reasons, I would never hear about it directly.

Of all the other Speakers in this quarter-century, there does not appear to have been a similar need or request. By far the greater volume of constituency help is in individual cases, and whether the problem is social services, immigration, or whatever, once a worthy case is brought to the attention of the Minister by any Member on any side of the House, with very few exceptions, the matter gets prompt and proper attention. The Speaker who had the greatest difficulty with impartiality was The Hon. René Beaudoin, but in everything recorded about that crisis, there was never any suggestion that he sought any extraordinary assistance from government for his constituency or, more interestingly, for himself. Even after his resignation, there wasn't the slightest hint that he had asked the Government to appoint him to anything. Actual experience seems to support the opposite view: that there is no connection between a Speaker's expectation of improved services to his constituency and his impartiality in dealing with the Government, and that if Speakers fall from the necessary level of objectivity, it is probably for other reasons. Of course, the fact that it hasn't happened so far doesn't mean that it never will.

In terms of mathematics, I was the 28th Speaker in 120 years since Confederation, and there were 265 seats in the House of Commons. The possibility of the same constituency going through this rather delicate relationship more than once in say 500 years is extremely remote, and all of the evidence shows that once it does occur, each individual constituency seems quite able to make the adjustment. Of course, I spent a great deal of time explaining the role of the Speaker, but on balance, probably no more than I did previously accounting to the voters in my capacity as a Member. In the nominating convention of 1979, my Liberal Party Association had to decide if it suited them to be represented in this way. The very same question was voted upon by the community at large in that general election. In both cases, there were a lot of questions and certain misconceptions which will never disappear entirely, but the understanding and the acceptance was likely as comprehensive as it was with the incumbent Members in the other 264 seats, neither more nor less. And so the argument runs: if all that is true and if going through the election process like any other Member seems generally to have been an asset for the Speaker rather than a liability, then why change it?

Turning again to the British experience, we must realize that they have been at this for four or five centuries longer than we have. Their practice has evolved very gradually and the designation of the Speaker on the election ballot is only one manifestation of it. Deputy Speakers are chosen from among senior Members with the care that befits the choice of a future Speaker and usually that is how it turns out. Unlike his Canadian counterpart, the British Speaker may sometimes step down in mid-Parliament and the House frequently elevates a recent Deputy Speaker to the position. Significantly, the mover and seconder of the Speaker's nominations at Westminster are not Party Leaders, but senior backbench Members from opposite sides of the House. As a result, after a short period of service, the British Speaker is always able to go to the polls as "Speaker Seeking Re-election," and normally continues through all of the following Parliament and part of the next, when the process is likely to be repeated. On retirement, now at an age where other appointments would be impractical, a Speaker goes only to the House of Lords, which eliminates even the appearance of speculation. In all of it, there is no sacrifice of the precept that the Speaker is a full-fledged elected Member of the House of Commons, like all the others. The Hon. Lucien Lamoureux tried to bridge the gap between Canada and Britain, and I think we all learned that, despite his efforts, it won't happen quickly and perhaps should not until either most of the elements of the British approach are accepted here, or else until all parties support some special arrangements for continuity in office.

Having thought through all of this, what about the concept of the permanent Speaker? As with the notion of the Speaker presenting himself as an independent candidate, my view on it has swung at one time or another to both extremes and now rests somewhere in the middle. There is a danger that any Speaker who doesn't have to answer to a constituency could become aloof—a procedural purist who might quickly bring the House to its knees—but most concepts of the permanent Speaker offset such a risk by requiring that the initial choice be made from among elected Members. There is also the safeguard that the option would not become available except with prior approval of the House, so there is always a graceful way to avoid prolonging the career of an unacceptable first choice by simply failing to put forward the necessary motion. With these controls, it is hard to imagine the House getting into great difficulty by keeping a Speaker for, let us say, five or six years after service in the first Parliament. For reasons which I am not quite able to explain, I have the feeling that this is an option Canadian Parliamentarians would find more acceptable than the British practice. But I honestly cannot see what harm could come from at least one experiment with it, and I hope that before too long our Parliament will find the time to study and debate some such proposal, which regrettably has never been done.

I certainly cannot leave this subject without reference to the very excellent work of the most recent Special Committee on Reform of the House of Commons under the Chairmanship of James A. McGrath, P.C. (St. John's). The central theme of their report tabled in June, 1985, is the frustration of the individual Member (as I have attempted to deal with it in chapter 4, "Games Members Play"). It is a very intelligent exploration of options to strengthen the independence and effectiveness of the back-bencher, without jeopardizing the principle of majority support, or confidence in the Government and the Prime Minister. I am impressed with the recommendations, but particularly that the House has already implemented several—one of which relates directly to the independence of the Speaker. As I understand it, the House has agreed to choose the next Speaker by secret ballot without prior nomination. That is an enormously important step in the right direction—the direction of removing even the appearance that the selection of a candidate for Speaker is the privilege of the Government. I look forward to the first use of it in a few years.

7. The First Commoner — Parliamentary Ambassador

The Speaker is often referred to as "The First Commoner," a designation which has survived over the years because it underlines two very important concepts. First, the Speaker is the representative of the entire House of Commons (indeed no other Member could do so without partisan overtone), and, second, all Members derive their status from their electorate and are therefore equal (although plainly, within each Parliament, and by the luck of the draw, some are "more equal" than others). It must never be forgotten therefore, that, although the Speakership has been described as "an honour in the highest gift of the House of Commons," the incumbent is never more than "first among equals." In this chapter, I want to share with you some of the agreeable experiences involved in carrying out that representative responsibility.

First of all, the extent to which this responsibility is shared with the Speaker of the Senate should be understood. Some of the internal administrative responsibilities, especially those for the benefit of the whole of Parliament—as for example the Parliamentary Library and the restaurant—are directed by committees of which the two Speakers are co-presidents. In a similar way, we shared a great many of what I call the diplomatic responsibilities. It is important to note here that the terms "House of Commons" and "Parliament" are not interchangeable. The Parliament of Canada consists of both the House of Commons and the Senate. Members of both Houses are *all* Members of Parliament. To be precise, the Monarchy is included in the concept of Parliament in the fullest sense, but for the moment suffice it to say that while each Speaker represents each House, it is entirely appropriate that the two Speakers should act together to represent Parliament.

It should also be remembered that Canadian protocol accords first position to the Governor-General, the Head of State who, on behalf of Her Majesty, brings legislation into being and expends the sums allocated by Parliament for that purpose. The second position goes to the Prime Minister, the elected political leader of the country and the person upon whose advice the Governor-General must act. The third position goes to the Chief Justice of the Supreme Court of Canada, who is also Deputy Governor-General. Positions four and five go to the Speakers of the Senate and the House of Commons, the higher position going to the Speaker of the Senate, since the Senators are the chosen advisors of the Governor-General, whereas Members of the House of Commons owe their primary obligation to their electors.

Before going further, let me say how profoundly fortunate I was to have served for five and half of my six years with The Hon. Madame Renaude Lapointe as Speaker of the Senate. I understand that over the years many other combinations were marred by a great deal of tension: but this delightful lady, a Quebec City career journalist, had a combination of intelligence, charm, wit, and personal warmth to make every moment of our shared duties an absolute pleasure for me. Whether we were co-hosts of an event on Parliament Hill, co-leaders of Parliamentary delegations in response to invitations from so many countries around the world, or at a Commonwealth Speakers' conference in London, she always displayed an interest and awareness of the problems under discussion, and managed to leave our guests or hosts very much enriched from having met her. I must add that in the too brief term of office of Senator Allister Grosart, her successor in 1979, and my good friend for many years, there was every appearance of carrying on the same very harmonious relationship, but events very quickly caused both of us to move on to other responsibilities.

There is considerable opportunity for Canadian Parliamentarians to come into contact with politicians from other countries, but I found on balance that it was neither more nor less than our counterparts around the world. In simple terms, attempting to assess the value of such international contact is no different than evaluating the importance of personal contact among our friends or neighbours, in our various associations, or in the world of business. The experience very closely parallels any other annual convention: putting a face, or more appropriately, a human being, with the written name; drawing comfort from shared concerns and uncertainties; making friendships that sometimes last a lifetime; always learning; and, in very many instances, opening informal avenues to solutions which could never be found at the negotiating table.

A great deal of this contact takes place within seven highly structured organizations. The two Speakers serve as honorary presidents of the Canadian branch of all of them. In terms of active involvement, it would be impossible for either Speaker to do justice to more than one or two of them. For me, the Commonwealth Parliamentary Association was an old and I suppose sentimental favourite because it was during my first trip outside Canada, to a C.P.A. conference in Australia in 1970, when Barry and I got the telephone call from Prime Minister Trudeau telling us of my appointment as a Parliamentary Secretary to the then Government House Leader, Allan MacEachen. The C.P.A. also sponsored the Commonwealth Speakers Association, which brought all the Speakers of Commonwealth Parliaments together every two years. The prime mover in the formation of the Commonwealth Speakers' Conference was Speaker Lamoureux, and he hosted the first conference in Canada in 1969. Speaker Lapointe and I had the honour of hosting the 1978 general conference.

I also took an equally active role in the Canada-United States Association, a personal indication of the importance I attach to the oldest and dearest friendship between our two countries. During my six years in office, I attended meetings in Washington and Ottawa, as well as in New Orleans, Calgary, and Quebec. My colleague Deputy Speaker Gérald Laniel balanced this with his very extensive participation in the two predominant French-speaking associations: Canada-France, and L'Association Internationale des Parlementaires de Langue Française. Let me quickly add, however, the very deep pride I felt in being presented with an A.I.P.L.F. award by their president Xavier Deneux. It was given to me as a tribute to my having become a bilingual Member of the House of Commons, and I cherish the medal very dearly. Learning French took me close to six years and of course

the learning process never stops, but it was worth every minute!
Here is a quick sketch of the seven associations:

Inter-Parliamentary Union:
Organized in 1889, it consists of groups from Parliaments of more than 95 member countries and is distinguished by the very high level of participation from the entire range of ideological, economic, and political systems. Obviously, "Parliamentary" is used in the generic sense, because many of the countries have other governmental systems, and many don't have what we would consider elected assemblies of any sort. I think it is this diversity that gives the I.P.U. its greatest value. The aims are to promote personal contact between individual members and to underline a commitment to international peace and cooperation by supporting the objectives of the United Nations. The Union headquarters is in Geneva and it meets in general conference in a different country every year. It also sponsors special meetings on security and cooperation, bringing together elected representatives from Europe, Canada, and the United States.

Commonwealth Parliamentary Association:
Originally founded in 1911 and renamed in 1948, its principal aim is to foster study and support for Parliamentary institutions. Each of the Canadian provincial legislatures is a member in its own right and, together with the territorial legislatures and Ottawa, Canada's 13 branches constitute one of seven regions in the Association. Within the Canadian region, there is an active programme of conferences and exchanges, including the Canadian Speakers' conference and an informational seminar for newly elected Members. I very much enjoyed personal contact with all of the Canadian Speakers and took great pleasure in hosting a dinner in Ottawa once a year as part of a conference where we were able to talk a little bit about the rather special experiences of our very tiny fraternity.

Canadian NATO Parliamentary Association:
Founded in 1955, its aim is to increase awareness of the concerns of the NATO member countries. Although independent, the North Atlantic Assembly is its related forum. With the opportunity for active participation in the spring and autumn sessions, and especially in the ongoing committees, Canadian Parliamen-

tarians are brought into intimate contact with our common defence obligations. Prior to becoming Speaker, I had the good fortune to serve on two Canadian NATO Parliamentary delegations, in Brussels and in Ankara.

International Association of French-Speaking Parliamentarians
This association was founded in 1967 and now has more than 30 sections. The headquarters is in Paris and a general assembly is convened every 18 months. Once again, within the Canadian region there is considerable interaction, particularly between Ottawa, the Quebec National Assembly, and the New Brunswick legislature, each of which are separate branches.

Canada-United States Inter-Parliamentary Group:
This group was founded in 1959, and normally meets annually with 24 delegates from the American Congress, the House of Commons, and both Senates. I think it is the best example of how truly beneficial these kinds of associations may come to be. Its beginnings were typical, and in the early years, the get-togethers were largely social (and probably lived up to the taxpayers' worst fears about politicians' junkets). Over the years, however, each side in turn developed a more serious attitude. By the early 1970s, the exchanges had achieved a very high quality.

The preparatory briefing sessions are now quite comprehensive. Every year, more and more substantial items are discussed, including such sensitive areas as cross-border television control, tax treatment of tourists, acid rain, Great Lakes clean-up, the proposed Garrison Dam diversion in the United States, fisheries, borders, Arctic sovereignty, and the law of the sea. Many of the members on both sides stay on through changes of administration, and I know that continued personal friendships have contributed immensely to the reduction of very serious tensions in all of these areas. Because of the importance of our close neighbour, and because of the already established level of participation in the other associations, Madame Lapointe and I attended almost every meeting, whether in Canada or the United States, in an attempt to personally underline the importance to Canada of this excellent association.

Canada-France Inter-Parliamentary Association:
Founded in 1965, this association's aim is to promote exchanges between French and Canadian Parliamentarians—primarily, of

course, French-speaking. The association meets once a year, alternating between Canada and France.

Canada-Europe Parliamentary Association:
The European Parliament at Strasbourg is the assembly for the member countries of the European Economic Community. Through this association, Canadian Members of Parliament are allowed to attend as observers and, from time to time, to participate in special meetings on bilateral issues of an urgent nature.

In addition to these groups, there are always a great number of special invitations to exchange visits with many countries around the world. Sometimes these special invitations are extended in the hope of gradually increasing the frequency of exchange, and even, ultimately, with a view to the establishment of new formalized associations. Speaker Lapointe and I headed a delegation to Japan in 1976, the culmination of dialogue which had been carried on for several years and which had begun with visits to Canada by a joint delegation of both Houses of the Japanese Diet. The exchanges gradually became more frequent, and there is now in place the Japan-Canada Friendship Association (which remains short of full official association status, but basically has all of the same aims and objectives). In almost exactly the same way, a similar sort of association developed with our other great neighbour on this continent: Mexico. The Mexicans have always been most anxious to increase contact, not only with us, but possibly in a tri-partite link with the United States. Other contacts of a similar nature rest at slightly less developed levels, as in the case of West Germany and Italy, and there is constant effort to do something similar with respect to a handful of other countries around the world.

Another pleasant surprise of the Speakership was that new diplomats to Canada included a visit to both Speakers when presenting their credentials. This always involved a very friendly half-hour chat, which gave me the opportunity for fresh insight into international affairs, and almost always included some suggestion of a Parliamentary exchange.

For both Speakers, evaluation of all of this participation is a very delicate matter. It includes allocating available funds between the various associations, scrutinizing their spending estimates, and deciding upon the encouragement of similar associations with other countries. I felt it required a kind of cross-party forum, so I invited suggestions in 1974 from the more experienced representatives of all existing associations. I am pleased to say not long after we were able to begin informal gatherings of the existing presidents of each of the associations, plus some of the past presidents and some senior staff from our Inter-Parliamentary Relations Secretariat. This informal advisory group was immediately of great help in assessing new proposals, but especially in the scrutiny of budgets and allocation of funds. There was another unexpected benefit a bit later: it has always been very difficult to try to arrange any kind of input from the Secretary of State for External Affairs about long range policy and priorities without giving the appearance of sacrificing the independence or autonomy of these associations. Now, by inviting the Minister to lunch with the Inter-Parliamentary Advisory Council, we were not only able to discuss matters openly, but for the first time to explore areas where both could function harmoniously without any loss of independence. The Inter-Parliamentary Advisory Council was of great assistance to both Speaker Lapointe and me. I hope it will continue to serve Speakers for many years to come.

My very first special invitation was presented to me by the head of our Inter-Parliamentary Relations Secretariat, Mr. Ian Imrie, within a few weeks of the opening of Parliament in 1974. It was a long-standing invitation to visit the Soviet Union, where an official visit from the Canadian Parliament had not taken place for almost ten years. I was, of course, fascinated at the prospect, but was not without some misgivings, especially since this was my first invitation. After a couple of discussions, it was obvious, given the schedule of House sittings, that the first date we could entertain with any certainty was almost a year away in September of 1975. As usual, Mr. Imrie opened up discussions with the Soviet Ambassador and his staff about all the details of the visit. Looking back, I draw some satisfaction in having insisted on two things: first, that our delegation would include a Ukrainian and a Jewish Member of Parliament; second, that we would be assured of some opportunity to discuss our concerns about communication and reunification between families. My idea was not to provoke conflict—far from it. I knew that it was to be a goodwill tour and that, as is always the case, it was never intended to be a vehicle for substantive discussions or for any kind of concrete negotiations.

But I did expect that the simple presence of these Canadian Members of Parliament would carry a message that wouldn't be lost on our hosts. I was sure that nothing of a more provocative nature would have to be done either before or during the tour and, happily, that is exactly the way it turned out, although not without some polite insistence on my part.

In making up such a delegation, Speakers usually first invite the party House Leaders and this was no exception. We also included Robert Kaplan (a Toronto Jewish Liberal) and Steve Paproski (a Ukrainian Conservative from Edmonton). We all enjoy reminiscing about the tour, particularly about one or two rather emotional moments. At a dinner in Kiev, capital of the Ukraine, I asked Mr. Paproski to respond to the toast to Canada, but not before I had first explained that his Ukrainian mother and Polish father had grown up only a few miles from Kiev, and that in this respect he represented a very significant force in Canadian life. We were especially pleased that he could speak on our behalf. A couple of days later, when the entertainment after lunch was a Dixieland jazz group, the same Steve Paproski got up on stage and joined them for a rendition of "Hello Dolly."

But the real excitement for me came after we had completed our tour, and had returned to Moscow. On the final day, we had meetings in the Kremlin, the afternoon session with Nikolai Podgorny, the late President of the U.S.S.R. Early in the day, it appeared that our hosts were prepared, as they had been at each stop along the tour, to use almost the whole time telling us of their accomplishments within the U.S.S.R., and to leave almost no time for discussions of the things we wanted to raise with them. I felt I had to interrupt to make sure that we could get on to these other topics. When we did, we got some unexpected drama. On the subject of unification of Jewish families, we gave the floor to Mr. Kaplan who became a bit emotional, and perhaps a bit more forceful than would normally suit a goodwill tour. He was interrupted by the co-leader of the meeting for our hosts, who began to berate us for attempting to tell them how to run their society. Our embassy people and the staff assigned to our tour from the Russian protocol office were beginning to get quite uncomfortable. So I gambled on intervening again and explained that not only was this not the forum for negotiation of diplomatic problems, but more than that, ours was a delegation of Parliament (indeed all parties of Parliament), and had nothing to do with Canadian government. As such, the Members in our delegation represented electors from all walks of life in every corner of Canada—electors who constantly raised these questions with us. Our purpose in raising them with the Soviets, therefore, was simply to give our hosts a better understanding of the kind of questions we would be asked upon our return. If they were hoping, as we were, for a more cordial relationship between our two countries in the future, then the Canadian electors and the Canadian Parliament would want to know what we were able to learn about Soviet attitudes toward such deep-seated concerns. Above all, we had neither the desire, nor would we presume to tell them how to manage their internal affairs. It all ended on a happy note and we went on to a magnificent formal lunch in the Kremlin. It was my first and certainly one of the most memorable moments in the international context of my years as a Speaker.

In Ottawa, the event that stands out most in my mind was when Her Majesty Queen Elizabeth II and His Royal Highness Prince Philip visited Canada in celebration of the 25th anniversary of her coronation in 1978. The trip included three days in Ottawa during which Mme Lapointe and I were the official hosts on behalf of Parliament. There was a reception and dinner in the Parliamentary dining-room during which I was seated next to Her Majesty, and Speaker Lapointe next to Prince Philip. Later, I had the pleasure of introducing Her Majesty to as many Members and Senators as were able to greet her personally during a one-and-a-half-hour walk-about in the Hall of Honour next to the main entrance to the Parliament buildings. During dinner, I touched on the subject of their children, particularly since Prince Andrew was at that time attending school in Canada, and because of the suggestion that Prince Charles might be invited by Australia to serve as Governor-General. Her Majesty's concern was that such a responsibility would be inappropriate until Charles was a bit older and probably married. Our conversation continued in a most natural and pleasant way, not much different than any other parents talking about their children.

Let me conclude this episode by sharing a little conversation that took place on the final day of Her Majesty's visit, when Senator Lapointe and I, attired in our formal garb, were waiting to receive the Royal couple at the head of the stairs of the entrance to Parliament. While we were chatting to pass the time, I asked her, now that she had been in the company of the Royal couple for the last three days, whether she would like to be Queen. With that ever-present twinkle in her eye, and the warmth of her French accent, I will never forget her reply: "Non merci—I would rather be the mistress of the Prince!"

One other delightful part of the Speakers' social responsibilities was when we held a party for the 100th anniversary of the Parliamentary Library in the Hall of Honour. It was attended by all the Members and Senators, and their guests, as well as the Governor-General. The party featured a cake baked by the head chef, Jan Van Dierendonck. The cake was a perfect replica of the Library building, and to this day, it remains on display in the Library.

I can't close off the subject of social responsibilities without at least a brief reference to a rather bizarre annual event that I likely supported more enthusiastically than any other Canadian Speaker—the annual Press Gallery dinner and show. The first of these evenings was held in 1948 and, at least at the time of writing, it was still not in great peril of discontinuance. It consists of a formal dinner in the Parliament buildings, followed by speeches from the political Party Leaders—all intended to be funny and, above all, guaranteed to be "off the record." I don't need to tell you that a great many of the speeches fell far short of the mark, but many, particularly Robert Stanfield's, were superb. A response is made by the president of the Press Gallery, who is expected to set the tone for what is to follow by putting the Party Leaders through the shredder. I must say the success ratio is very high. What follows is a collection of musical skits, usually with a connecting theme, but uniformly with one purpose in mind: to lampoon the prominent political figures of the day.

One of the first times I thought I stuck my neck out a bit for this group was in the spring of 1975. The theme was Prime Minister Trudeau's swimming-pool and they asked (and I think were a little surprised to get my blessing) whether they might actually put up a backyard pool in the Railway Committee Room. The show was opened by Gallery member Iain Hunter dressed in a kilt doing an imitation of Mr. Stanfield playing the bagpipes. As Mr. Hunter attempted to exit gracefully from the stage he fell right in the water, bagpipes and all. He swears it was unplanned. I suppose the whole thing appealed to me because my mother and father met in the vaudeville days of the Grand Theatre in Kingston—she was singing on stage and he was playing in the pit orchestra. I also firmly believe that the best thing that can happen to politicians, especially pompous ones, is to find out that at least once in awhile no one is being fooled. Nothing in any of the dozen or so annual performances that I have seen has done anything to change that view. I have also had the pleasure of sharing the stage with them at fund-raisers in aid of performing arts, including two huge successes for the Sudbury Theatre Centre. Like most of my colleagues in the House, I hope many of them will remain life-long friends.

8. The Decision to Leave

Almost no one leaves political life voluntarily. Simplistic, I suppose, but quite true, and hardly surprising considering the astronomical odds against getting a party nomination and then winning an election. This is not to say that the turnover is small —quite the reverse. In my first general election in 1968, there were 265 seats and one hundred of us were new faces and that ratio has been about the average since Confederation. In fact, the number goes considerably higher if the election produces a change of Government, or if one or two Party Leaders have changed. A handful of senior Members do decide to go on to other responsibilities, but otherwise the casualties occur entirely at the hands of the voters.

Prior to 1974, I was not conscious of the role played in it by the Speaker. It is the Speaker who announces the resignation of any Member to the House. Before doing so, of course, steps must be taken to be quite sure that the resignation is intentional and not a sort of whimsical step that the Member might want to retract after a few days. For that reason, the Member must submit a letter of resignation to the Speaker. It has been the practice to have it attested by two witnesses, usually other Members of the House. Before announcing any resignation, I always made it a point to have a chat with the resigning Member, of course, but also to personally verify the signature of both witnesses.

My first experience with a voluntary resignation came as quite a shock. Scarcely six months after my election as Speaker, Hon. John Turner sought an appointment with me to bring the appropriate letter along. Here was a high profile political star, one of those Cabinet Ministers who had come to Sudbury to help me campaign in my 1967 by-election. I had never thought of Parliament without John Turner being a part of it, but I relate this here for another reason. During our conversation, he said something I didn't fully comprehend until six years later. His resignation from Cabinet over a disagreement of course was not easy, but it was nothing at all compared to the agony of having to give up his membership in the House of Commons.

Over the years, even the most highly motivated of Members will be forgiven for getting caught up in the political dog fights—and perhaps losing sight of the more important relationships within Parliament. I can tell you that it is only when you sit down for the first time, as I did in December of 1979, and realize that you are about to leave it for good, that the full impact of the honour of representing the people of your community in Parliament really hits home.

In a fascinating way there is a problem to getting out of political life that is nearly as puzzling as getting in. I call it "the dilemma of power," but however you may want to describe it, this is how it comes about. Members who spend some time in Opposition do so always in the hope of getting into power. When the party is in power, the hope is to get into Cabinet, but if that happens, an odd sort of trap begins to close. At first, of course, the idea of getting out of political life is the farthest thing in the mind of the new Minister, but down the road, when the first thoughts of leaving begin to creep in, a painful reality emerges. Those very Cabinet Ministers who routinely approve appointments for hundreds of other people can almost never do so for themselves. There is simply never a time that the political party can be comfortable with what appears to be people abandoning ship. Everyone's motivation has to be constantly onward and upward to an even greater victory in the next election. But when defeat inevitably arrives, tragically, they are never in a position to consider looking after themselves until it is too late. Just scan the newspapers after a general election, especially where there has been a change of Party Leader or a change of Government, and look for the stories of former Members, many of whom were Cabinet Ministers, suddenly adrift, attempting to re-establish their identity in the "real world."

This brings me to a couple of other pet personal theories about political life—both of them probably unrealistic in the real world.

In my opinion, we lost something when we crossed the line into politics as a full-time or lifelong career in its own right. I realize that the enormous responsibility placed upon our political leaders is no longer something that can be discharged on a part-time basis. However, that doesn't prevent me from believing that some of the smaller Canadian provinces, as an example, are closer to the way politics was intended to be. Their legislatures sit a few weeks—perhaps once or twice a year. Members of the community are elected and participate in the governmental process in the full sense, but their identity as a member of the community remains paramount: as housewife, lawyer, teacher, or whatever. Their personal identity doesn't totally dissolve into the political world.

I also think it would be far better to have a limit on the number of years that people might serve in public office—not, heaven forbid, because I think that those great veterans with long years of service are not dedicated and capable, far from it. But I would be prepared to sacrifice that possibility in favour of this principle. People should be conscious that it is a role or service they will render for a time and that, eventually, they must go back to the community. I think it would help them maintain perspective and independence, and be better elected Members because of it. I know that the chances for all of this have long since gone by, but I wish they hadn't.

In an odd sort of way, one compensation of the Speakership is the escape from the power dilemma. In the earlier chapters of this book you will recall my great misgivings about taking on the Speakership. One of the main reasons for my resistance was because I knew it was a step that would lead me out of political life, and it did. It isn't that my decision to leave in 1979 became any easier, but it certainly was more predictable. It gave me a lot of time to think about it and, indeed, I did just that more or less constantly during all of the six years. Still, the decision involved a whole range of emotional forces greater than I had ever experienced. I don't think they can be understood without touching upon the extreme highs and lows of political life.

For the high points, turn to any page of this book! The whole story is really all about the high side. Being the Speaker of the House of Commons absorbed more of my time, energy, and constant attention than anything I had ever done before, but I loved every minute of it! How could I possibly single out any one moment or aspect it: my first election to the House of Commons, my first speech, my election as Speaker the first time, the second time, hosting royalty here in Canada, being received like royalty all around the world, living at magnificent Kingsmere in a lifestyle that money cannot buy. . . . Does any of that exceed the warm satisfaction of a thank you for replacing a lost pension cheque, arranging a flight home for an injured child on a National Defence aircraft when parents had no hope of doing it on their own, or a gift of a personal family treasure to symbolize gratitude for the unification of a family? Is it more memorable than watching the construction of a huge Taxation Data Centre, knowing that the resulting employment will bring desperately needed balance to Sudbury's economy long after I am gone?

Perhaps I can illustrate it best with reference to two events that were so symbolic of the highest moments. The first was an honorary LL.D. conferred on me by the University of Toronto at the convocation of my old alma mater, St. Michael's College, in 1980. The degree was, of course, a great honour, but in his presentation address, Father John Kelly, a beloved fixture around the college ever since I had been there as an under-graduate, said something I didn't expect and won't soon forget. He said that one of the reasons for my selection had been that as an English Canadian I had made a contribution to Canadian unity by learning French and by using it daily in the House of Commons and that it should serve as an example to many unilingual Canadians. If there is any truth in that, is there any other walk of life where such an opportunity can be found?

The second event was a testimonial dinner for me in Sudbury in June of 1980. When I first heard about the plans, I was thrilled, but as I thought about it, I really began to worry about how it would be if only a few people turned up, especially since it was during Sudbury's bleakest economic times. Of course, I wouldn't be telling the story if it wasn't a happy one. The dinner was held in the Caruso Club, the Sudbury Italian Community Hall, where we had held many of our political meetings, nominating conventions, and particularly our victory celebrations. Every ticket had been sold, every seat filled. It was a great tribute. But it wasn't so much who or how many people were there as how they felt. It was a genuine celebration. There was an unmistakable atmosphere of friendship, even affection. There were 700 people there and I knew everyone of them. Most had not only voted for me, but had worked for me in every campaign. But a great many were of other political persuasions. A number of new friends from Ottawa were there too. The head table represented the three parties in Parliament, and at Queen's Park, along with Archbishop Carter and a number of Sudbury community leaders. Dan Newell, publicity chairman for all my campaigns, was Master of Ceremonies. He insulted and roasted all of the visiting dignitaries in his own inimitable fashion—certainly much more fun for the audience than it was for the head table! The last of the tributes was from the floor and given by John Hartman, one of the first people we had met on arrival in Sudbury many years ago. In reply, I had thought of saying so many things (many of which I never had the chance to fully express until I wrote this book), but I confined it to one basic theme, which I want to stress here. More than anything else, it is the reason why I have told the story about this dinner. I knew that evening that I was among friends and that as I said goodnight to them individually, and I did, I could look them in the eye and know that if they had anything to do with my 13 years as their Member of Parliament, they never had to hang their head about it. Can anyone really ask anything more?

There are low points too. There is a terrible price that goes with political life. In our case, during the first seven years, it was the disruption of our normal family life. There are obvious strains upon a Member, but they are no greater, perhaps less so, than on the wife and mother of small children. In our case, Barry, who thought that being uprooted from her family to come to Sudbury initially was the biggest hurdle she would have to bear in our marriage, found herself ten years later up to her neck in the strange world of political campaigns, only to learn that one of the fruits of victory was for her to stay home, run the house, and raise the children, while I played my V.I.P. role in Ottawa. Then, when I did get home on weekends, often as not, she would find herself both evenings at gatherings (sometimes at more than one event a night) to which we had some sort of obligation, and, just for good measure, there would be a thorough going-over on an open-line show or in the weekend papers. The adverse publicity is no pleasure for the Member, but I think it really hurts wives in a much more sensitive way.

Unhappily, the alternative is no better. Attempting to uproot everybody into some kind of rented accommodation in Ottawa would have been all wrong—to say nothing of taking Barry and the children away from all of their friends. And, as a political consideration, the people of Sudbury would have been appalled at the idea. In my case, it might have been worth a try had there been any hope of a sitting schedule that coincided with school months. While that was every year a topic of optimistic conversation amongst Members, it never happened until after I left. The House always sat into July, sometimes August, and then would resume in mid-October. What arrangements could anyone hope to make regarding the children's school schedule, unless they were resigned to spending the whole 12 months in Ottawa? The fact is that by the time we had come to the 1974 election campaign, I knew that this couldn't go on much longer, particularly since we were coming into the teenage years. I had pretty much come to the conclusion that either there would be greater involvement in Ottawa, as in Cabinet, or else I would simply spend more time in my Sudbury law practice, and keep my time in Ottawa to the minimum necessary to do a proper job. The fact that we would again be together under one roof all of the time was a major factor in my decision to accept the Speakership in 1974.

I must say the Kingsmere experience surpassed even our greatest expectations. During the 1974-75 term, I lived in the apartment provided right next to the Speaker's office and continued to commute on weekends so that Barry was able to stay in Sudbury for the birth of our fifth child, Megan, at the Sudbury General Hospital on November 28, 1974. During the remaining five years, we lived at Kingsmere, the former summer residence of Prime Minister Mackenzie King, which he willed to the government as a Speaker's residence. At Kingsmere we were provided with a staff that included a chauffeur and cook, and for entertaining, we could call upon the entire hospitality staff of the House of Commons. Kingsmere is in the Gatineau hills just directly north of the City of Ottawa, in the Province of Quebec. It sits on several hundred acres of beautiful rolling terrain that is an absolute paradise in every season. And yet, even with all of this, it was always understood that the day I decided to stop would be welcomed by Barry with unrestrained joy! In retrospect, I suppose there could hardly be a better test of the agony of that decision to leave, because the lifestyle certainly gave us every excuse not to step down.

Was there a symbolic all-time low? Let me take you to December 13, 1976. For two years I had been battling, at the request of the then Mayor of Sudbury, to help in a cause that I thought was hopeless for us—the forthcoming Canada Summer Games. I say it seemed hopeless because we were then in the midst of our success on the Data Centre and I didn't think we would be favoured with two such blessings in such a short space of time. However, as often happens, through a curious combination of luck and timing, other sites were unacceptable to either the provincial or federal Ministries, and by default we fell into a situation where the Minister (Hon. Iona Campagnola) made a verbal commitment to Sudbury. In fact a meeting to put together the details was taking place that morning between our three executive assistants, when the Mayor, quite on his own and without as much as informing me in advance, took it upon himself to tell the Minister that he was afraid Sudbury might not be able to afford the Games. It's a good thing we were 300 miles apart, because I wanted to strangle him on the steps of City Hall!

Before that settled down, I heard that a delegation of Sudbury Union leaders, was on its way to see the Secretary of State for External Affairs about seabed mining. Later in the day, that meeting took place while I was locked in the House attempting to sort out a two-hour procedural wrangle. As I stepped out of the Chair to return to my office, I got a telephone call that I pray no parent ever receives. In the fierce afternoon snowstorm, our four children had been driving through the City of Hull on their way home to Kingsmere and were hit head-on by a vehicle that had jumped the median. The only serious injury was to our son Joey who was in the back seat and had his face pressed against the window which shattered, ripping the skin off half his face. We spent the rest of that day, in ambulances and hospitals, waiting for the plastic surgeon to give us the final verdict, at first not knowing if he would survive, or lose his eye. For ten days Barry stayed with him in the daytime and I slept in his hospital room at night. Need I tell you that more than once during that time my only thought was that if I hadn't been in politics and particularly if the children hadn't been driving to the Speaker's residence, none of this would have happened. That Christmas of 1976, I wished I had never had anything to do with any of it. (Incidentally, Joey made a great recovery.)

There was one other totally unexpected element in the decision to leave. In late 1978, Prime Minister Trudeau announced his resignation and the Liberal Party called a Liberal Convention for March of 1979. For quite a while, there was great speculation that either Donald Macdonald or John Turner would be the next Leader, but it seemed quite certain that they would not run against each other; and at one time or another, both made very definite announcements that they would not run. An entirely unexpected and an interesting spin-off from all of that was the rather wide-ranging speculation on which other English Canadian bilingual Liberal might be the logical successor in the absence of both Macdonald and Turner—and some of the speculation included me. After one particularly complimentary article by Allan Fotheringham (who certainly was never renowned for his generosity of spirit in these sorts of things), the speculation really intensified. I began to joke that if I could have Marc Lalonde and John Turner as my campaign managers, and Paul Desmarais and Conrad Black as my finance chairmen, I would consider running. But even that actually began to trickle back to me, and during the days leading up to Christmas, it was obvious that a number of people were taking it seriously. What worried me was the thought that perhaps I was among them. However, before matters got out of hand, the Clark government was caught in a surprise defeat in December, and Mr. Trudeau agreed to stay on and indeed went on to win a majority government in the February 18 election. Hindsight, of course, is perfect vision and events had answered the question for me, so I didn't have to make the choice on my own. What a colossal mistake it would have been had I taken so much as one step to indicate my interest in political leadership. In a single stroke, I would have destroyed any credibility that I enjoyed and set the Canadian Speakership back half a century. Please accept this: I do remember that one of the factors in my decision was that when I began to believe those kinds of rumours, I knew it was certainly time for me to leave.

In any case, this all comes to the decision of December, 1979. Friends watching the proceedings on television said that I had a look of disbelief on my face that was plainly visible as I stood in the

Chair to announce the result of the vote, which Prime Minister Clark accepted as a defeat of his government the following morning. Indeed, I was astonished because I didn't understand any of the elements of the defeat and I was totally surprised that it had happened. I suppose more than anything else it underlined the ultimate madness of elected Members putting their lives at the mercy of this process every few years, and, often, every few months.

But the decision to leave was more than a reaction to negative factors—much of it had a very positive overtone. Very few people have the good fortune to get into a career they really enjoy. In 1979, I knew that before too long I would be starting on my third thoroughly enjoyable career, and I was anxious to get it under way. In 15 years as a lawyer, I had always felt it would be a great honour to serve on the Bench—all the more fascinating if it could be in a different discipline from the jury practice I had known. The exact timing, then, was influenced, indeed dictated, by the existence of the opportunity to serve on the Court created by the Federal Parliament in 1972 and, in the intervening years, assigned responsibility for a wide range of emerging areas of the law. On February 18, 1980 I was sworn in as Associate Chief Justice of the Federal Court of Canada.

Trying now to re-create the sensations that went with stepping down, I remember three: fatigue, of course, to the point almost of numbness, but a couple of days of sleep took care of that; then relief—throughout it all, I knew that no matter how good it all was today it could always blow up in my face tomorrow, so in that sense I was glad it was finally over.

The final sensation is not one I can really categorize. I found myself strolling (not rushing) through a downtown Sudbury mall crowded with Christmas shoppers. When I saw the Salvation Army Santa Claus and a couple of trumpet players playing carols, I went up behind them and put some money in the pot. I didn't walk around in front of them so they would see who it was, and I didn't try to attract attention from the crowd by shaking hands with the Santa Claus. Only if you have spent a few years in public life can you understand what a huge difference that makes.

If I could turn the clock back 20 years knowing what I do now, would I do it all again? Absolutely.

Index

49, 51, 55, 76, 83, 89, 103, 114, 116, 117, 120, 122, 124, 126, 130, 131, 149, 153, 162, 164
House of Commons Language School, 48
House Order of January 25, 1977 (television coverage), 115-116, 117
House pages, 129-132
House pages' 5th Anniversary Dinner, 131-132
Hunter, Iain, 158

Imrie, Ian, 155
International Nickel Company (INCO), 109, 139
Inter-Parliamentary Advisory Council, 155
Inter-Parliamentary Relations Secretariat, 155
Inter-Parliamentary Union, 152
Irving Pulp and Paper, 107
Italy, 154

Japan-Canada Friendship Association, 154
Japanese Diet, 154
Jerome, Mrs. James, 15, 16, 17, 18, 20, 25, 30, 47, 48, 129, 151, 165, 166, 167
Jerome, Jim Jr., 15
Jerome, Joey, 15, 167, 168
Jerome, Mary Lou, 15
Jerome, Megan, 15, 48, 166
Jerome, Paul, 15
Joint Committee of the Senate and the House of Commons (illegal drug use), 115
Justice and Legal Affairs Committee, 22, 28, 31, 34

Kaplan, Robert, 156
Kelly, Father John, 164
Kingsmere, 16, 48, 50, 164, 166, 167
Knowles, Stanley, 69, 110, 134, 135, 142
Koester, Dr. Beverley, 12, 74, 127
Kremlin, 156, 157

Lalonde, Marc, 168
Lambert, Adrien, 92, 107
Lambert, Speaker Marcel, 23
Lamoureux, Speaker Lucien, 23, 27,

29, 30, 31, 114, 133, 134, 135, 137, 139, 140, 141, 142, 143, 145, 147, 151
Laniel, Gérald, 12, 13, 151
Lapointe, Mme. Renaude, 115, 150, 151, 153, 154, 155, 157, 158
LaSalle, Roch, 78, 79
Late Show, 26, 60, 63-64, 68
Lawrence, Allan, 28, 101, 102, 109
Lawson Graphics, 14
Lefebvre, Mr., 93
Léger, Mlle. Annette, 132
Léger, Jules, 42
Lenthall, William, 41, 42
Liberal caucus, 47, 138, 143, 144
Liberal Party, 27, 141, 168
Laballister, David, 14
Laundy, Philip, 14
Leggatt, Stuart, 29

MacDonald, David, 63
Macdonald, Donald S., 22, 25, 27, 28, 168
MacDonnell, James, 125, 126, 127
MacEachen, Allan, 25, 26, 77, 79, 84, 151
MacEachen budget (1983), 47
Mace of the House of Commons, 43-44, 49
MacGuigan, Mark, 29
MacKay, Elmer, 82, 83, 84, 95, 96
Mackenzie King, William Lyon, 166
MacNaughton, Speaker, 22
Macrillo, Sam, 65
Malone, Mr., 80
Maloney, Arthur, 13
Martin, Keith, 67
Martin, Paul, 20
Mazankowski, Don, 65
McCleave, Robert, 32
McDonald Royal Commission (R.C.M.P.), 101, 104
McGrath, James A., 148
Mexico, 154
Michener, Roland, 135
Miller, Maki and Inch, 18
ministerial responsibility, 97
minority Parliament of 1979, 12, 145
Mitchell, Roger, 19, 121
Monarchy, 44-45, 149
More, Sir Thomas, 41
M.P.s' support services, 26, 123

DATE DUE
DATE DE RETOUR

APR 1 1 1987			